THE SHOOTING SCRIPT®

CORIOLANUS

SCREENPLAY BY JOHN LOGAN

BASED ON THE PLAY *CORIOLANUS* BY WILLIAM SHAKESPEARE

INTRODUCTION AND NOTES BY JOHN LOGAN

FOREWORD BY AND Q & A WITH RALPH FIENNES

newmarket press
for itbooks
AN IMPRINT OF HARPERCOLLINS PUBLISHERS

D1291988

A Newmarket Shooting Script® Series Book

Printed in the United States of America.

No part of this book may be used or reproduced in any manner whatsoever without written permission except in the case of brief quotations embodied in critical articles or reviews. For information address HarperCollins Publishers, 10 East 53rd Street, New York, NY 10022.

Books may be purchased for educational, business, or sales promotional use. For information address HarperCollins publishers, 10 East 53rd Street, New York, NY 10022.

First Edition

Library of Congress Cataloging-in-Publication Data is available upon request.

ISBN 978-0-06-220257-4
12 13 14 15 16   10 9 8 7 6 5 4 3 2 1

The Newmarket Shooting Script® Series is a registered trademark.

CONTENTS

FOREWORD

BY RALPH FIENNES

It's intriguing to speculate how Shakespeare might have responded to Film. I believe he would have relished its possibilities: the narrative power of film editing, the interior life transmitted in the landscape of a close-up and the illusion of reality—of life and actors photographed—makes one think he would have seized all of a filmmaker's tools to hold the "mirror up to Nature."

But what of the spoken word—the unique, expressive range of thoughts and feelings contained in the spoken language of Shakespeare's characters? Film distrusts and often resists complex and rich speech. The history and development of filmmaking have increasingly refuted and rejected anything thought to have its roots in the theatre. Would Shakespeare have contracted and simplified speech for Film? We'll never know. But, John Logan and I share a belief in Shakespeare's language keeping its impact and beauty within a modern filmic context.

John's screenplay has done something extraordinary—in its potent and visceral filmic description, it takes the reader/viewer into an immediately recognisable modern world. He takes us dynamically through the story of *Coriolanus* with great visual force and judges beautifully the impact of the spoken word—Shakespeare's speech—unafraid of its power and its challenge. The challenge to open the ear alongside the eye.

There would be no film of *Coriolanus* without John's belief in this confrontational, jagged tragedy as a piece of cinema. Whatever "pitch" I proposed to him, I knew it would be nothing without a strong, clear screenplay. The first draft, arriving only seven weeks after we thrashed out some essential ideas for cuts and setting, was urgent, filmic, and utterly true to the spirit of Shakespeare. John's film-sense and his strong narrative instinct, embracing the power of the spoken word, have resulted in a screenplay that's a page-turner in its own right. A pleasure to read in itself.

It gave a first-time director the chance and learning of a lifetime. Gratitude knows no bounds.

—London, December 2011

INTRODUCTION

BY JOHN LOGAN

I am a writer today because of Shakespeare.

When I was about eight, my father insisted I watch a movie with him on television. It was a sunny Southern California day outside, and I didn't want to stay in the gloom of our small den watching a movie, especially with my very un-cool Dad. I whined and tried to escape. He finally wooed me by saying, "It's got ghosts and a swordfight." Being a great fan of both ghosts and swordfights, I relented. The movie was Laurence Olivier's version of *Hamlet*. Something shifted in my life that afternoon and I've never been quite the same: I was Shakespeare-struck. Here was the most exciting swordfight I had ever seen on screen (still is) in the midst of a mysterious, frightening story, and all expressed with language every bit as thrilling as the flashing rapiers.

My father—a naval architect from Belfast, who always loved literature—encouraged my growing obsession with all things Shakespeare. We read the Lambs' *Tales from Shakespeare* and then dipped into some of the actual plays, starting with those that featured sword fights. So I was introduced to *Coriolanus* at an unhealthy early age. Of course, I had no capacity to even begin understanding the complexity and majesty of the plays, but that didn't matter. It was Shakespeare's unparalleled storytelling and the vibrancy of his characters that took hold and would not let go. Later I would learn to appreciate the joyously synapse-flashing exuberance of the language, the dazzling neologisms, the seemingly endless supply of poetry.

So it was a Shakespeare movie that eventually led me into the rest of my life in the theatre.

Once I starting writing screenplays, it was inevitable I would eventually hurl myself at a Shakespeare. And it was always *Coriolanus* in my mind. To me there is something uniquely modern and cinematic about the play. Not necessarily because of the obvious contemporary parallels and resonances: military figure moving into government; the pressure of the media and keeping popular support; the compromises of the political process; the realities of modern warfare; the economic decline of a Superpower. What makes Shakespeare's play so terribly contemporary and cinematic to me is the grim and lonely complexity of the title character: he invites the searching close up like Charles Foster Kane or T. E. Lawrence in *Lawrence of Arabia*. Coriolanus is similarly opaque and unknowable; he's neurotic, violent, degraded, and ennobled simultaneously. He is purely and austerely himself. Until finally he is subsumed by his own story and his very humanity disappears: "Coriolanus/ He would not answer to; forbade all names;/ He was a kind of nothing." (V. i) Is he the first post-modern character in literature?

Now, as you might imagine, not many people shared my particular obsession with bringing this challenging, blood-soaked, and unbeloved late Shakespeare play to the screen. After all, it's not exactly *Romeo and Juliet*. But it turns out one man did share my passion, a man every bit as Shakespeare-struck as myself. Even more so. Before I met Ralph Fiennes I was skeptical. My agent had told me he was interested in making his directing debut with a film of *Coriolanus*. Beyond the sheer insanity of such a venture, I suspected an actor's vanity project and approached our first meeting with a very healthy respect for his work and an equally healthy hesitation.

However, within ten minutes of meeting him, I knew I was going to make the movie with Ralph. He spoke with knowledge and insight—and the lunatic passion that is the first requirement of a true filmmaker. He could not be deterred; there was something deep inside the DNA of the play he needed to express and transform through cinema. Most importantly, we saw precisely the same movie in our heads: relentless, modern, and as uncompromising as Shakespeare's play. That first day we resolved to do it. There was no deal, there was no money, there was no studio. We just did it. I called my agent and told him I was going to be unavailable for a while.

For a long while it turned out. At 3824 lines, *Coriolanus* is Shakespeare's second-longest play; only *Hamlet* is longer. Uncut, the play in performance runs close to four hours. So the first task facing us was bringing the mammoth text down to a manageable length. Having recently cut an hour from Stephen Sondheim's great score of *Sweeney Todd* for the film version, I was very aware of the particular anguish of cutting material you love. What I learned from that experience is the only way to make such severe cuts is boldly. Be smart about it, know the text backwards and forwards, and remember you're making a movie, not filming a stage performance. My feeling about adapting *Coriolanus* was always this: Shakespeare's play has been around for four hundred years, and will be performed four hundred years from now; nothing I can do is going to harm his great play. This helped give me the confidence to be nervy with the adaptation.

As Ralph and I explored the play, an organizing principle emerged for the film version: *keep the focus on the protagonist.* Master dramatist that he is, Shakespeare wrote a play about a ferocious warrior whose climax depicts not a battle, but a son weeping in his mother's arms. It is a harrowing family drama as much as anything. We wanted to examine that vexatious family in all the depth we could and with all the tools of cinema: probing into the most private corners and darkest rooms. So elements of the text that were more tangential to Coriolanus' personal story began to fall away. The more "public" elements of the play having to do with the people of Rome, the politics, and the military situation were cut to keep the "private" and psychological story central.

Working from this basis, over several months, gradually the spine of the movie emerged. There was never a doubt that every word spoken in the film would be from Shakespeare's play, and we wanted to let some of that language truly breathe. We knew we couldn't be afraid of the longer speeches or soliloquies. To allow these linguistic explosions we had to create moments of cinematic composure or stillness about them. But even with that, I sought to play the active verbs more than the ruminations or poetry. I purposefully tried to write the screenplay to be as verb-filled and agile as I could to suggest the energetic, propulsive movie Ralph and I envisioned. Short jabs, not long caresses.

After doing sixteen drafts—yes, fellow screenwriters, take a breath—sixteen drafts, the script was ready to go. I've rarely enjoyed the process more. Ralph was a marvelously committed, respectful, and responsive director. He was tireless in reading my drafts and offering his thoughts and insights at every step. In a way, ironically, I think we were both trying to recreate the feeling of being in rehearsals for a new play: experimentation; constant engagement; willingness to play and to make mistakes; to be bravely bad.

We got into the guts of Shakespeare's play side-by-side and emerged with a movie of which we are both inordinately proud. On the day we wrapped, I asked him: "So when do we start on the next one?"

Sadly, my father died shortly after we wrapped, so he never got to see the finished film. But I know he was especially proud I was doing it. My secret hope for the movie is that someday some kid somewhere will be forced to sit with his very un-cool father and watch *Coriolanus*.

And maybe he'll get Shakespeare-struck.

—London, November 2011

CORIOLANUS

by

William Shakespeare

Screenplay

By

John Logan

The blade of a knife.

Pulled from its sheath, intricate tribal etchings on the
blade catching the light.

The blade being pulled across a sharpening stone. Swoosh-
swoosh-swoosh. Rhythmic. A well-practiced hand. A muscular,
tattooed arm.

The blade held up. Razor sharp. The glow of a TV in the
darkened room is the only illumination.

We see images on the TV:

GLOBAL AND URBAN STRIFE ... slums ... barricades ... poverty
... starvation ... demonstrations ... repression ... refugee
camps ... barbed wire prisons ... riot police ... tear gas
... violence...

Then the images settle to now, BREAKING NEWS:

FOOD RIOTS IN ROME. Images of a protest march. A crowd
filling the streets. Soldiers moving into position. We see
placards: "DOGS MUST EAT," "MEAT WAS MADE FOR MOUTHS."

The man sharpening the knife watches the images. His eyes are
cold. Almost disinterested.

Then he stops.

Frozen in mid-stroke.

Something on the TV suddenly <u>rivets him</u>.

His eyes no longer cold.

The TV shows one of the soldiers, a high-ranking officer.
Imperious. Giving orders. We will come to know this is a man
as Caius Martius -- Coriolanus.

<u>TULLUS AUFIDIUS</u>, the man sharpening the knife, gazes at the
image on the screen.

He leans forward. Emerging from the darkness. We see his
face.

He is a handsome and imposing figure, magnetic in his
personality. Charismatic, yes, but also neurotic and edgy.
Uncomfortable in his own skin. Some demons there.

He watches the face of Caius Martius on the TV screen.

Then he puts the point of his knife against the screen.
Against Caius Martius' heart.

Holds it there ... Presses the point against the screen ...
Muscles knotting in his forearm ... As if he could thrust the
knife through the screen and into the heart of Caius
Martius...

His nemesis ... His dark angel.

Sharp cut to--

2   EXT. ROME - STREET - DAY   2

We move with an intense woman down the street. She is
nervous. Checks she is not being followed.

She is <u>TAMORA</u>, an extreme figure on the political landscape.
To the Roman elite she is a dangerous anarchist -- to her
supporters she is an ardent patriot and democrat.

As she moves, we take in Rome.

It might be Mexico City. Or Chechnya. Or El Salvador. Or
Detroit. Or Baghdad. Or London.

This Rome is a modern place. It is <u>our</u> <u>world</u> <u>right</u> <u>now</u>:
immediately recognizable to us. Elements of classical
architecture loom over decay. Monolithic modernism and brave
public monuments are lost in a sea of brazen advertising
billboards, neon shopping plazas and drab super-highways.
Splendor and squalor sit side-by-side.

It is a volatile, dangerous world.

William Shakespeare's Rome.

She comes to a graffiti-covered apartment building. Looks
around. Enters.

3   INT. APARTMENT - DAY   3

A secret political meeting in a police state.

Tension. Cigarette smoke hangs in the air. Men and women
gathered, hushed and urgent tones. A cell meeting of the
political opposition, the resistance.

A TV shows the food marches elsewhere in the city. The
gathering storm.

CASSIUS is a leading proletariat organizer:

>   CASSIUS
>   Before we proceed any further, hear me
>   speak -- You are all resolved rather to
>   die than to famish?

The others agree. They are not wild-eyed radicals. They are
normal people, from all walks of life. You and me.

>   CASSIUS
>   First, you know Caius Martius is chief
>   enemy to the people.

A voice from the back of the room:

>   TAMORA
>   Let us kill him.

The others turn. Tamora, just entering, pulls off her coat,
joins the others:

>   TAMORA
>   And we'll have corn at our own price. Is
>   it a verdict?

Some are unsure. She is too extreme for some.

>   CASSIUS
>   (pressing slightly)
>   We are accounted poor citizens, the
>   patricians good ... The leanness that
>   afflicts us, the object of our misery,
>   our sufferance, is a gain to them. Let us
>   revenge this with our sticks ere we
>   become rakes! ... I speak this in hunger
>   for bread, not in thirst for revenge.

A woman, a YOUNG MOTHER, protests:

>   YOUNG MOTHER
>   Will you proceed especially against Caius
>   Martius?

>   CASSIUS
>   Against him first.

A COLLEGE PROFESSOR, speaks up:

>   COLLEGE PROFESSOR
>   Consider you what services he has done
>   for his country?

                    TAMORA
               (snaps)
          Very well, and could be content to give
          him good report for it -- but that he
          pays himself with being proud.

                    COLLEGE PROFESSOR
          Nay, but speak not maliciously.

She has over-played her hand. Pretends to back down:

                    TAMORA
          I say unto you, what he hath done
          famously, he did it to that end...
               (a snarky smile)
          He did it to please his mother.

Some laugh at her gossip.

Then the TV image switches to a BREAKING NEWS update:

From the Roman Senate. An august press room. A Senator is
moving to a podium to make a statement.

He is Senator MENENIUS, a seasoned and wily politician.
Silver hair, perfectly tailored suit. He is known as a folksy
"man of the people." It is a role he plays to perfection.

                    CASSIUS
          Soft, who comes here?

                    COLLEGE PROFESSOR
          Worthy Senator Menenius, one that hath
          always loved the people.

                    TAMORA
          He's one honest enough; would all the
          rest were so.

                    MENENIUS
               (on TV)
          Why, masters, my good friends, mine
          honest neighbors,
          Will you undo yourselves?
               (smiles benevolently)
          I tell you, friends, most charitable care
          Have the patricians of you,
          For your wants,
          Your suffering in this dearth, you may as
          well
          Strike at the heavens with your staves as
          lift them
          Against the Roman state--

                         TAMORA
                   (speaking to the TV)
              Suffer us to famish, and their
              storehouses crammed with grain--

The others shush her.

                         MENENIUS
                   (on TV)
              Alack, you are transported by calamity
              Thither where more attends you; and you
              slander
              The helms of the state, who care for you
              like fathers,
              When you curse them as enemies--

Cassius mutes the TV. We see Senator Menenius continuing with
his speech; his attempt to calm the dangerous situation.

                         CASSIUS
              Care for us? They never cared for us yet!

                         TAMORA
              If the wars eat us not up, they will: and
              that's all the love they bear us.

The others are growing increasingly restive -- shifting --
tension building--

                         CASSIUS
              Why stay we prating here?

                         TAMORA
              No more talking on it!
              To the Capitol! Come! Come!

Cut to--

4   EXT. STREETS - DAY   4

Tamora, Cassius and the others are now in the midst of the
protest march. The crowd has become a mob, with a life and
will of its own. The crowd surges toward some towering grain
silos in the distance--

They round a corner and suddenly stop--

For a formidable sight awaits them--

RIOT POLICE.

Rows of black uniforms. Full riot gear with plexiglass shields and dangerous truncheons.

The crowd starts and shifts nervously, unsure how to proceed. Should they launch themselves against this monolithic military force?

A long, tense beat.

Then...

The riot police part and CAIUS MARTIUS steps forward. (He is soon to be given the honorary title Coriolanus.) He is intense and patrician. Uncompromising. A man of steel. A soldier. He wears a crisp, military uniform.

He slowly walks to the mob...

With no hesitation, unarmed...

The crowd watches his approach closely ... Some are in awe at being so close to this hero of Rome ... For others, it's odd. They came to kill him, but he's offering himself. Something about him holds the crowd back.

Martius stops before Cassius...

His manner is direct, quiet. Stating facts.

> MARTIUS
> What's the matter, you dissentious
> rogues,
> That, rubbing the poor itch of your
> opinion,
> Make yourselves scabs?

> CASSIUS
> (sarcastic)
> We have ever your good word.

> MARTIUS
> He that will give good words to thee will
> flatter
> Beneath abhorring.

The crowd is hushed. Taking in his every word.

We note a TV news crew has moved into position and is filming eagerly. Some in the crowd film with cell phone cameras. Streaming video. *We intercut some of these perspectives.*

> MARTIUS
> What would you have, you curs?
> He that trusts to you,
> Where he should find you lions, finds you
> hares;
> Where foxes, geese.

He is not declaring. He's calm. He walks along the front of
the crowd. Some are frightened by the great Martius. Some in
awe. Others glare at him with loathing.

> MARTIUS
> Who deserves greatness
> Deserves your hate...
> Hang ye! Trust ye?
> With every minute you do change your
> mind,
> And call him noble that was now your
> hate,
> Him vile that was your garland.

His eyes take in face after face:

> MARTIUS
> What's the matter,
> That in these several places of the city
> You cry against the noble Senate, who,
> Under the gods, keep you in awe, which
> else
> Would feed on one another?

He stops and takes in the whole crowd.

His sheer sense of command is unmistakable.

An ultimatum:

> MARTIUS
> Go ... Get you home, you fragments.

A tense beat.

The riot police shift nervously.

The crowd is unsure.

The TV news crew films everything.

Cassius looks around. He sees the police ready with tear gas.
He sees old men, women and children in his crowd. He doesn't
want this to explode.

He exchanges a few whispers works with Tamora. Word is passed and the crowd begins to disperse. The police move in to clear stragglers. Some run off in a panic. Others walk away.

The danger has passed.

Senator Menenius stands by his limousine nearby.

He gestures for Martius to join him. He is an old family friend of Martius' as well as his mentor and chief political advisor.

5   INT. LIMO - DAY   5

Martius and Menenius sit in the back of the limo as it creeps along. Menenius is relieved bloodshed has been avoided.

                    MENENIUS
          These are almost thoroughly persuaded;
          For though abundantly they lack
          discretion,
          Yet are they passing cowardly.

                    MARTIUS
          They are dissolved. Hang 'em.

Senator Menenius watches the crowd through the window. Disturbed.

                    MENENIUS
          I would they were abed.

                    MARTIUS
          I would they were in Tiber.

6   INT. DARKENED ROOM - DAY   6

We see the TV image of Martius speaking to the people:

                    MARTIUS
                 (on TV)
          Go ... Get you home, you fragments.

Tullus Aufidius is leaning in. Watching so closely.

From his POV: the pixelated close-up of Martius' face on the screen.

He runs his knife blade back and forth. Turns it in the light; the reflection of Martius' face distorting as he rotates the blade.

Then Aufidius leans back again.

Back into the shadows. Disappearing.

7   INT. CATACOMBS - NIGHT   7

Aufidius, who is the leader of the rebel Volscian forces, is
striding, deep in thought.

The Volsces are an insurgent force challenging the monolithic
might of Rome: rebels that suggest to us Latin American
revolutionaries or Hamas fighters or Chechnian separatists.

They are a dangerous guerilla force.

Aufidius weaves through the dank and claustrophobic catacombs
beneath an ancient building. Dripping water. Graffiti.

His OFFICERS and some civilian POLITICIANS struggle to keep
up with his quick gait:

                    VOLSCE POLITICIAN
          So, your opinion is, Aufidius,
          That they of Rome are entered in our
          counsels
          And know how we proceed.

                    AUFIDIUS
               (snaps)
          Is it not yours?
          Tis not four days gone since I heard
          thence.

                    VOLSCE OFFICER
          We never yet made doubt but Rome was
          ready
          To answer us.

                    VOLSCE POLITICIAN
          And it is rumored Martius, your old
          enemy, leads in their preparation.

Aufidius' eyes spark at the name. He continues with a
strange, grim fire:

                    AUFIDIUS
          If we and Caius Martius chance to meet,
          'Tis sworn between us we shall ever
          strike
          Till one can do no more.
          By the elements,
                    (MORE)

                          AUFIDIUS (cont'd)
          If ever again I meet him beard to beard,
          He's mine or I am his.

He strides into a cellar room. Heavily-guarded. The
politicians are stopped outside. They are not welcome here.

8   INT. CATACOMBS-CELLAR ROOM - DAY   8

Aufidius enters the cramped chamber.

A few Volsce soldiers. All with their faces covered with ski
masks. An old, stained mattress and a half-eaten plate of
food.

One soldier is setting up a video camera. Turns on its
blinding light to reveal--

A young ROMAN SOLDIER. Kneeling. Head bowed, bloody. He's a
prisoner. Tied up. We see a dog tag around his neck. He looks
up into the bright video camera light. Blinks. Scared.

The video camera hums. Recording the event.

The Young Soldier knows exactly what's about to happen.

                          YOUNG SOLDIER
          Please...

                          AUFIDIUS
          Know you me yet?

                          YOUNG SOLDIER
          I know you well. Your name I think is
          Aufidius.

                          AUFIDIUS
          It is so.

                          YOUNG SOLDIER
                    (desperate)
          I am a Roman!

He begins to cry.

                          AUFIDIUS
          What's the news in Rome?

The Young Soldier looks around. Will anyone help him?

The masked faces staring back are unnerving.

                          AUFIDIUS
          What's the news in Rome?

The Soldier doesn't answer. Aufidius draws his elaborately etched knife. The Young Soldier understands the threat.

>   YOUNG SOLDIER
>   There have been in Rome strange
>   insurrections ... The people against the
>   Senators.

>   AUFIDIUS
>   "Hath been?" Is it ended then?

>   YOUNG SOLDIER
>   The main blaze of it is past but a small
>   thing would make it flame again.

Aufidius looks at him. Considers this.

A long beat. The video camera hums. The Young Soldier stares.

>   AUFIDIUS
>   You have ended my business.

He turns to go but--

With sudden ferocity he spins back to the Young Soldier -- grabs the Soldier's head -- yanks it back -- and slashes his throat--

HARD CUT TO--

9   INT. ROMAN WAR ROOM - DAY   9

On a TV screen:

The terrible image from the video -- the Young Soldier, head yanked back, throat slashed -- the atrocity searing the consciousness of Rome--

The TV image is paused.

Martius is seated with several MILITARY OFFICERS and AIDES.

Also with him is TITUS. He is younger than Martius, an old friend and comrade-in-arms. Like Martius he has seen a lot of battle.

COMINIUS, an older general, enters. He is an experienced commander of men also used to dealing with the necessary politics of civilian oversight. West Point bearing.

All salute. Cominius returns the salute.

COMINIUS
The news is the Volsces are in arms.

An aide presses a remote. Grainy video images play on a
computer screen: Volscian soldiers, jeeps, tanks.

One section shows a quick image of Tullus Aufidius riding
past in a jeep.

COMINIUS
They have a leader,
Tullus Aufidius, that will put you to it.

MARTIUS
I sin in envying his nobility,
And were I any thing but what I am,
I would wish me only he.

SENATOR
You have fought together?

MARTIUS
He is a lion
That I am proud to hunt.

Martius takes the remote control. Stops the video. Rewinds to
the unclear image of Aufidius.

MARTIUS
Titus Lartius, thou
Shalt see me once more strike at Tullus'
face.

Martius rewinds and plays the image of Aufidius again,
rewinds and plays it again, almost obsessively.

We push in on the video image of Aufidius.

Aufidius appears to be staring right back at Martius.

10   EXT. MARTIUS VILLA - DAY   10

A beautiful butterfly. Catching the light perfectly, almost
iridescent.

It floats before a palatial mansion in the suburbs of the
great city. Manicured lawns. Formal gardens. Classical
architectural lines.

This fine home of aristocratic privilege seems a world away
from the urban blight of Rome.

In the immaculate front gardens <u>YOUNG MARTIUS</u>, Martius' son, is target shooting. BANG. Aims again. BANG. Something a little cold about him.

We realize he is being observed...

11   INT. MARTIUS VILLA -- LIVING ROOM - DAY   11

... <u>VIRGILIA</u>, Martius' wife, stands at the window.

Virgilia was well-chosen for her role as wife to one of Rome's most aristocratic men. She is beautiful and graceful but -- like Diana thrown into the lion's den of the Windsor family -- woefully out of her depth. We feel an inner fragility to her.

The room is spacious and elegantly appointed. A lovely Roman statue in one corner. This is a place of wealth, order and control.

A fine flat-screen TV flickers with images of war. We see helicopters zooming over desert landscape ... Imbedded war correspondents ... Tanks ... Combat ... Romans ... Volscians.

<u>VOLUMNIA</u>, Martius' mother, stands and watches the TV. She is an imposing woman, handsome and tall, impeccably dressed. Adamantine in her strength.

Virgilia moves from the window. Sits on a sofa. She watches the TV news footage of the war, upset by the images.

A frozen silence.

Then:

> VOLUMNIA
> I pray you, daughter, sing, or express
> yourself in a more comfortable sort. If
> my son were my husband, I should more
> freely rejoice in that absence wherein he
> won <u>honor</u> than in the embracements of his
> bed where he would show most love.

She moves across the room. She moves, always, with stately grace.

She walks past a series of photographs. They tell the story of Martius' life: the happy baby; the stern dead father; the rigid young military cadet; the formal wedding; the restrained and unsmiling adult.

In the photos we sense a transformation: innocent boy to experienced, severe looking soldier. Volumnia is present in most of the pictures.

As:

> VOLUMNIA
> When yet he was but tender-bodied and the only son of my womb, I, considering how honor would become such a person, was pleased to let him seek danger where he was like to find fame ... To a cruel war I sent him, from whence he returned, his brows bound with oak.

> VIRGILIA
> But had he died in the business, madam, how then?

> VOLUMNIA
> Then his good report should have been my son.
> (she rivets Virgilia)
> Had I a dozen sons I had rather have eleven die nobly for their country than one voluptuously surfeit out of action.

A MAID enters. She speaks to Volumnia (the true mistress of the house) not to Virgilia.

> MAID
> Madam, Senator Menenius is come to visit you.

> VOLUMNIA
> Tell Menenius we are fit to bid him welcome.

The Maid goes.

> VIRGILIA
> Beseech you, give me leave to retire myself.

> VOLUMNIA
> Indeed, you shall not!

She turns off the TV and goes to a bar to mix drinks. She mixes the drinks aggressively, strangely inspired by the discussion of war:

                    VOLUMNIA
        Methinks I hear hither your husband's
        drum;
        Methinks I see him stamp thus, and call
        thus:
        "Come on, you cowards! You were got in
        fear,
        Though you were born in Rome." His bloody
        brow
        Then wiping, forth he goes.

                    VIRGILIA
        His bloody brow? O Jupiter, no blood...

                    VOLUMNIA
        Away, you fool! It more becomes a man
        Than gold his trophy.

                    VIRGILIA
        Heavens bless my lord from fell
        Aufidius...

                    VOLUMNIA
        He'll beat Aufidius' head below his knee
        And tread upon his neck.

Senator Menenius enters, he is comfortable in this house and
an old ally of Volumnia's.

                    MENENIUS
        My ladies both, good day to you.

Volumnia hands him one of the drinks she has been mixing: a
perfect martini. She knows how he takes his drink. She is not
above flirting with him when it suits her ends.

                    MENENIUS
        How do you both?
            (to Virgilia)
        And how does your little son?

                    VIRGILIA
        I thank you, sir; well, good.

                    VOLUMNIA
        He had rather play with swords and hear a
        drum than look upon his schoolmaster.

                    MENENIUS
        On my word, the father's son!

He and Volumnia laugh.

Menenius has sensed Virgilia's tension. Tries to cheer her:

                    MENENIUS
          Come, I must have you play the idle
          housewife with me this afternoon.

                    VIRGILIA
          No, good sir, I will not out of doors.

                    MENENIUS
          Not out of doors!

                    VOLUMNIA
          She shall, she shall.

                    VIRGILIA
          Indeed, no, by your patience. I'll not
          over the threshold till my lord return
          from the wars.

                    MENENIUS
          Fie, you confine yourself most
          unreasonably.

                    VIRGILIA
          I cannot go hither.

                    MENENIUS
               (playfully)
          You would be another Penelope; yet they
          say all the yarn she spun in Ulysses'
          absence did but fill Ithaca full of
          moths.

                    VIRGILIA
          No, good sir, pardon me; indeed, I will
          not forth.

                    MENENIUS
          Go with me and I'll tell you excellent
          news of your husband.

                    VIRGILIA
          O, good sir, there can be none yet.

                    MENENIUS
          There came news from him last night.

Volumnia pounces, moving in:

                    VOLUMNIA
          Indeed?

Menenius consults his Blackberry:

                    MENENIUS
          Your lord and Titus Lartius are set down
          before the Volscian city of Corioles.
          They nothing doubt prevailing and to make
          it brief wars ... This is true, on mine
          honor; and so, I pray, go out with us.

                    VIRGILIA
               (again declining)
          Give me excuse, good sir. I will obey you
          in everything hereafter.

                    VOLUMNIA
               (snaps)
          Let her alone. As she is now, she will
          but disease our better mirth.

She takes Menenius arm and pulls him out, eager for more news
of her son.

Virgilia sits for a beat.

Then she presses a button on the remote control. The TV goes
on again. More news reports of the war.

We see images of the Volscian town of Corioles. A "BREAKING
NEWS" scroll runs across the bottom of the screen ... The
Battle for Corioles ...

Virgilia watches the war footage, her eyes haunted.

Hard cut to--

12   EXT. CORIOLES - DAY   12

BLAM! BLAM! BLAM! A series of explosions jolt us.

Corioles is a small urban center. Smoke billows up from areas
of the city. The steady crack and rattle of gunfire. The
occasional thud of explosions.

We see urban street-to-street fighting. The images are
startling in their familiarity: this could be Basra or
Belfast.

The battle is photographed in a gritty exposure. Color is
drained out -- blood is a darker red like oil. Soldiers are
dark forms moving through shadows and smoke.

Martius and Titus, leading a platoon of around twenty Roman SOLDIERS, run into view and take cover. Bullets zip and snap around them.

The Roman soldiers wear modern battle fatigues and body armor, tricked out with all the latest tech gear. The Volscians, being a poor guerilla force, wear thrown together uniforms that look almost tribal.

Martius calls over the incessant din of battle to Titus and the soldiers:

> MARTIUS
> They fear us not, but issue forth their
> city.

Sniper bullets slam into a wall near him. He coughs away the smoke and debris. This only makes him more angry:

> MARTIUS
> They do disdain us much beyond our
> thoughts,
> Which makes me sweat with wrath!
> He that retires, I'll take him for a
> Volsce,
> And he shall feel mine edge!

Martius leaps up and races on. The others follow in military order.

The Roman soldiers move along the street -- it is chaotic -- explosions, smoke and sniper fire -- they duck into doorways and behind abandoned cars -- returning fire as best they can--

Martius leads -- firing stead bursts from his machine gun--

It is slow and bloody going--

Finally the Romans turn a corner and are stopped by a roadblock: a burning bus that fills the entire street--

The Volsces use this roadblock to ambush the Roman soldiers--

We see glimpses of Volscian soldiers darting for position -- firing from rooftops and from inside shops--

Blistering crossfire--

13   INT. BLASTED HOTEL ROOM - DAY   13

Aufidius runs into a blasted hotel room. Some of his soldiers with him.

He goes to the window. Scans the street below. Sees Martius and the others trapped at the bus. He gestures to an aide for a radio--

14   EXT. CORIOLES-STREET - DAY   14

In the face of the crossfire, the Roman soldiers start falling back--

Martius refuses to yield -- pushing and shoving his men toward the burning bus -- screaming in fury over the noise:

> MARTIUS
> You souls of geese,
> That bear the shapes of men! PLUTO AND
> HELL!
> All hurt behind! Backs red, and faces
> pale
> With flight and agued fear! Mend and
> charge home,
> Or, by the fires of heaven, I'll leave
> the foe
> AND MAKE MY WARS ON YOU!

An EXPLOSION -- dirt and brick shards slash across Martius' face -- blood--

This only pushes his fury to white rage--

> MARTIUS
> Look to it. Come on!
> FOLLOW ME!

He leaves his soldiers behind--

Moves alone to the burning bus and fights his way through the flames--

Martius is in his own world now. He doesn't even realize he is alone. He has become a sort of killing machine. A shark moving through the ocean. Ruthless and efficient.

We become the warrior.

From Martius' POV:

We move through disorienting curtains of smoke...

Continue down the street...

Firing a heavy machine gun...

Volscian soldiers contort and die, torn to pieces by the bullets...

The heavy machine gun is empty, we drop it and use a sidearm, firing strategic shots...

Volscian soldiers dart up -- fire -- and die...

We keep moving steadily forward...

Shadowy shapes moving nearby, we fire. Killing civilians. The fortunes of war...

Strange surreal images. We smash into a house. An OLD MAN crouches, terrified, in a corner. He reaches forward. He is offering us water. An act of kindness amid the violence...

We move on...

Panicked civilians, scattering in terror...

Volscian soldiers rush us, attacking, we slam them aside...

We duck down, roll under a car, emerge and fire...

More Volscians die...

We continue forward...

Then the pistol is empty, we drop it and pull a machete-like knife...

Still moving relentlessly forward...

Slashing and killing...

Hand-to-hand now...

Carnage.

15   EXT. CORIOLES-ALLEY - DAY   15

Aufidius and his aides are racing down an alley, trying to get to Martius--

Roman fire stops them--

They return fire as they divert down another alley, trying for a better strategic position, running flat out--

16   EXT. CORIOLES - LATER   16

Titus and the soldiers are still pinned down at the burning
bus. Two soldiers race back to Titus to report, they dive for
cover.

                    TITUS
          What is become of Martius?

                    SOLDIER 1
          Slain, sir, doubtless.

                    SOLDIER 2
          He is himself alone,
          To answer all the city.

                    TITUS
          Thou art lost, Martius...

Titus has no time to mourn. He looks over the hopeless
situation. Scanning the rooftops, windows and shops.

Then he stops ... He sees something ... Past the burning bus
... Through the smoke and flames...

He glimpses a ghostly figure...

                    TITUS
          Who's yonder,
          That does appear as he were flayed? ...
          O gods! He has the stamp of Martius.

It is indeed Martius.

A shocking sight.

Drenched head-to-toe in blood.

His face splattered with gore.

His eyes wild.

Lost in something like rapture.

                    MARTIUS
          Come I too late?! ... Come I too late?!

                    TITUS
          Ay, if you come not in the blood of
          others,
          But mantled in your own.

SUDDENLY -- a deafening explosion -- and RPG EXPLODING from nearby. Then gunfire. Bullets shatter windows. The Volscians are attacking again.

The Romans instantly begin diving for cover and taking up defensive positions--

Martius scans the location. Sees the attack is coming from an old Hilton hotel. Now pockmarked with bullets and artillery shells. Most of the windows shattered.

This is the Volscian stronghold. The last stand. He sees flashes of Volscian soldiers moving on the roof and balconies, and snipers firing from windows.

There is an open plaza, littered with bodies and debris, in front of the hotel.

Martius stops scanning with his binoculars--

Sees Aufidius moving in the hotel, directing the battle--

>   MARTIUS
>   There is the man of my soul's hate--
>   Aufidius--
>   Piercing our Romans.

>   TITUS
>   Worthy sir, thou bleeds.
>   Thy exercise hath been too violent
>   For a second course of fight.

>   MARTIUS
>   Sir, praise me not.
>   My work hath yet not warmed me.
>   The blood I drop is more medicinal
>   Than dangerous to me. To Aufidius thus
>   I will appear and fight.

He turns to some soldiers, imploring them to join him. His bloody visage and intensity are strangely inspiring, his ferocity infectious:

>   MARTIUS
>   (to soldiers)
>   If any such be here-
>   As it were sin to doubt - that love this
>   painting
>   Wherein you see me smeared; if any fear
>   Lesser his person than an ill report;
>   If any think brave death outweighs bad
>   life,
>   And that his country's dearer than
>   (MORE)

>   MARTIUS (cont'd)
>   himself;
>   Let him alone, or so many so minded,
>   Wave thus, to express his disposition,
>   AND FOLLOW MARTIUS!

The soldiers are pumped up -- like Marines straining for combat--

>   MARTIUS
>   O, ME ALONE! MAKE YOU A SWORD OF ME!

They bolt--

Zigzagging across the plaza toward the hotel--

Titus and the others provide covering fire--

17   EXT. CORIOLES-PLAZA - DAY   17

Martius zigzags with his men across the dangerously exposed plaza--

They return fire at the hotel as best they can, but the barrage from the Volscians is murderous--

Roman soldiers contort and fall, blood spraying--

Bullets snap and ricochet everywhere around them--

But still they keep up a steady pace, reloading and firing as they go--

Then Martius is hit--

Blood sprays--

But still he keeps on--

The front of the hotel is closer now--

Martius and his soldiers race to the hotel and crash into the lobby--

18   INT. CORIOLES-HOTEL-LOBBY - DAY   18

Martius and his soldiers battle the Volscian defenders in the hotel lobby--

It is the weird and incongruous nature of modern urban warfare: soldiers fighting to the death among hotel couches and tatty corporate artwork--

It is brutal--

Martius and his soldiers cut a bloody swath across the hotel lobby--

Another HUGE EXPLOSION rocks the hotel -- like a seismic blast -- an ugly 1970's chandelier falls--

Martius and his men move into a stairwell--

19   INT. CORIOLES-HOTEL-STAIRWELL - DAY   19

Martius and his men race up the stairway--

Volscians are firing down at them--

Bullets ricochet crazily in the confined stairway, refracting from concrete walls and twisting metal railing, sending up sparks and clouds of dust--

Then Martius slows to a stop.

Looks up.

Aufidius is on the stairway above. Glaring down at him.

A long beat as they lock eyes. Both panting for breath in the heat of the combat.

                    MARTIUS
          I'll fight with none but thee, for I do
          hate thee.

                    AUFIDIUS
          We hate alike.

Then Martius does something astounding.

He holds out his arms to his sides and drops his weapons. They clatter down.

Aufidius does the same.

The Roman and Volscian soldiers watch.

None daring to interfere.

Martius and Aufidius continue to glare at each other -- dropping weapons -- disarming -- Martius climbing up the stairs, Aufidius coming down -- moving closer and closer--

At an instant--

They slam together--

Fighting without weapons--

Grappling brutally. Tearing at each other. Twining together.
Fingers grasping. Teeth snapping. Hands pulling.

It is a bloody, terrible, graceless struggle.

They crash and slam awkwardly in the claustrophobic
stairwell. Smashing into the walls. Falling from level to
level--

Then--

Another EXPLOSION rocks the hotel--

Part of the roof COLLAPSES--

Concrete SLAMS down--

A cloud of smoke, dust and debris obscures everything--

Martius is tossed violently to the ground in the action--

Aufidius is pulled away by several of his men. They drag him
to safety. Roman soldiers fire after them. The sound is
deafening in the confined garage.

But Aufidius and his comrades disappear into a cloud of dust.
Gone.

Martius glares after him. Wipes blood from his eyes.

20   EXT. CORIOLES-STREET - NIGHT   20

Aufidius and some of his Volscian soldiers, bloody and
filthy, are on foot.

They are moving through the outskirts of Corioles, leaving
the city. Exhausted after the long and failed battle.

Fires burn from blasted shops and homes. The Romans have
clearly laid waste to this part of the city.

There is a minivan stopped ahead of them. Bullets holes
everywhere. Bodies inside.

They walk to it. Aufidius looks in. A dead family. Father,
mother, kids in the back. Bloody toys on the floor of the
minivan.

Roman atrocities.

Aufidius gazes at the bodies. His face hardens.

He whispers to himself:

> AUFIDIUS
> Five times, Martius,
> I have fought with thee; so often hast
> thou beat me,
> And would do so, I think, should we
> encounter
> As often as we eat.

He becomes aware some of his men are looking at him,
disturbed at his fervor.

> AUFIDIUS
> For where
> I thought to crush him in an equal force,
> True sword to sword, I'll stab him some
> way,
> Or wrath -- or craft -- may get him.

> SOLDIER
> He's the devil.

> AUFIDIUS
> Bolder, though not so subtle.

A beat. Aufidius continues with prayer-like intensity:

> AUFIDIUS
> My valor, poisoned with him,
> Shall fly out of itself...
> Nor sleep, nor sanctuary, being naked,
> Sick, the prayers of priests,
> Nor times of sacrifice,
> Shall lift up their rotten privilege
> And custom,
> Against my hate to Martius.

In the shattered glass of the minivan window, Aufidius
suddenly sees himself.

He studies his own face, nurturing his dark thoughts.

> AUFIDIUS
> Where I find him, were it
> At home, upon my brother's guard, even
> there,
> Will I wash my fierce hand in his heart.

INT. POLITICO BAR - DAY

Back in Rome, we are at a comfortable restaurant/bar near the
Senate where politicians gather to eat, drink, gossip and
conspire. The business of state is conducted over steak and
martinis.

Comfortable red leather booths. Wooden panelling.

Two Tribunes -- Senators chosen to speak for the people --
are having lunch.

BRUTUS is a large man in a rumpled grey suit; a sweating bear
with a taste for bare-knuckle politics. SICINIUS is smaller
and vulpine; crafty and cold.

Both are ambitious politicos used to manipulating the people
and the press for their personal ends. With them sits
Cassius, the political agitator we met before.

The TV over the bar shows images of Martius' victory:
parading Roman troops; Volscian prisoners; flags; adoring
crowds; triumphant slogans; "Mission Accomplished."

                    SICINIUS
          Was ever man so proud as is this Martius?

                    CASSIUS
          He has no equal.

                    SICINIUS
          When we were chosen Tribunes for the
          people-

                    BRUTUS
          Marked you his lip and eyes?

                    SICINIUS
          Nay, but his taunts.

They see Senator Menenius approaching. Sicinius nods to
Cassius, who quickly goes.

Menenius stops by on his way out. He is jolly, knowing the
victory will assure his protege's political future:

                    MENENIUS
          The augurer tells me we shall have news
          tonight.

                    BRUTUS
          Good or bad?

                    MENENIUS
          Not according to the prayer of the
          people, for they love not Martius.

                    SICINIUS
          Nature teaches beasts to know their
          friends.

                    MENENIUS
          You blame Martius for being proud?

                    BRUTUS
          We do it not alone, sir.

Subtly, the polite chit-chat is turning more serious and
pointed; Menenius growing sharper. The gloves are coming off.

                    MENENIUS
          I know you can do very little alone ...
          You talk of pride: O that you could turn
          your eyes toward the napes of your necks,
          and make but an interior survey of your
          good selves! O that you could!

                    BRUTUS
          What then, sir?

                    MENENIUS
          Why, then you should discover a brace of
          unmeriting, proud, violent, testy
          politicians, alias fools, as any in Rome.

The saturnine Sicinius' response seems almost a threat:

                    SICINIUS
          Menenius, you are known well enough too.

                    MENENIUS
          I am known to be a humorous patrician,
          and one that loves a cup of hot wine with
          not a drop of allaying water in it; one
          that converses more with the buttock of
          the night than with the forehead of the
          morning. What I think I utter, and spend
          my malice in my breath.

                    BRUTUS
          Come, sir, come, we know you well enough.

                    MENENIUS
          You know neither me, yourselves nor
          anything ... You are ... <u>ambitious</u>.

A tense beat. They are formidable adversaries.

> MENENIUS
> Good-e'en to your worships. More of your
> conversation would infect my brain, being
> the herdsmen of the beastly plebeians ...
> I will be bold to take my leave of you.

He goes. The Tribunes watch him cut through the lunch crowd
and exit.

21 EXT. HOUSE - DAY   21

Volumnia, Virgilia, Young Martius and Menenius emerge from
the house and head toward the waiting limousine. All are well-
dressed, for an important public event.

> VOLUMNIA
> Honorable Menenius, my boy Martius
> approaches! For the love of Juno, let's
> go.

> MENENIUS
> Is he not wounded? He was wont to come
> home wounded.

> VIRGILIA
> O, no, no, no...

> VOLUMNIA
> (victoriously)
> O, he is wounded! I thank the gods for
> it.

> MENENIUS
> So do I too -- if it be not too much.
> Brings a victory in his pocket, the
> wounds become him. Has he disciplined
> Aufidius soundly?

> VOLUMNIA
> Titus Lartius says they fought together,
> but Aufidius got off.

> VIRGILIA
> In truth, there's wondrous things spoke
> of him. Gods grant them true.

> VOLUMNIA
> (an exhalation of scorn)
> True?!

                    MENENIUS
        I'll be sworn they are true. Where is he
        wounded?

Volumnia and Menenius now gleefully add up her son's wounds
like accountants -- or campaign managers.

                    VOLUMNIA
        In the shoulder and in the left arm.
        There will be large scars to show the
        people, when he shall stand for his
        place. He had, before this last
        expedition, twenty-five wounds upon him.

                    MENENIUS
        Now it's twenty-seven. Every gash was an
        enemy's grave.

They climb into the limo.

22   EXT. SENATE - DAY   22

The Roman Senate is constructed with classical symmetry and
clean, square lines. Probably the most striking and beautiful
building in Rome.

We see Martius' boots. Slowly moving up a long stairway. Each
step measured and difficult.

Soldiers flank him.

23   INT. SENATE-STAIRS - DAY   23

Volumnia, Virgilia, Young Martius and Menenius are waiting
with Cominius and other dignitaries at the top of a majestic
stairway.

An honor guard of Roman soldiers in dress uniforms are
waiting. Roman flags flutter. All very ceremonial.

Martius enters below. The honor guard snaps to attention.

Martius -- hereafter called Coriolanus -- slowly begins to
cross to the steps. We see that walking is very difficult
for him. His wounds are severe and every movement is agony.

He has paid a steep price for his victory.

Photographers flash photos and a TV crew film the ceremony.

Coriolanus finally reaches the steps leading up. He takes a breath and slowly begins to climb the stairs, each step a challenge.

Volumnia looks down on him. Unmoved by his pain.

We focus on her face:

>   VOLUMNIA (V.O.)
>   Before him
>   He carries noise, and behind him he
>   leaves tears.
>   Death, that dark spirit, in his nervy arm
>   doth lie;
>   Which, being advanced, declines, and then
>   men die.

As Coriolanus slowly hauls himself up the last few steps, General Cominius speaks into a cluster of microphones and addresses the press:

>   COMINIUS
>   Be it known,
>   As to us, to all the world, that Caius
>   Martius
>   Wears this war's garland ... And from
>   this time,
>   For what he did before Corioles, call
>   him,
>   With all the applause and clamor of the
>   host,
>   "Caius Martius Coriolanus!"
>   (to Martius)
>   Bear the addition nobly ever!

The soldiers salute in a grim sort of chant:

>   SOLDIERS
>   Caius ... Martius ... Coriolanus!

Coriolanus has reached the podium. An awkward beat. Cominius gestures for him to speak into the microphones.

He tersely does so:

>   CORIOLANUS
>   No more of this; it does offend my heart.
>   Pray now, no more.

An awkward silence. Cominius elegantly tries to covers the moment:

                    COMINIUS
          Look, sir, your mother.

                    CORIOLANUS
          O,
          You have, I know, petitioned all the gods
          For my prosperity.

He kneels to her -- slowly, with great difficulty -- she lets
him.

                    VOLUMNIA
          Nay, my good soldier, up.
                  (he slowly rises)
          My gentle Martius, worthy Caius, and
          By deed-achieving honor newly named -
          What is it? - Coriolanus must I call
          thee?

She laughs coquettishly, thoroughly upstaging her son.

Then, almost an afterthought:

                    VOLUMNIA
          But, O, thy wife...

Coriolanus greets Virgilia with an awkwardly tender kiss.

                    CORIOLANUS
          My gracious silence, hail.

He notes her tears. Reacts with unexpected gentleness.

                    CORIOLANUS
          Would thou have laughed had I come
          coffined home,
          That weeps to see me triumph? Ay, my
          dear,
          Such eyes the widows in Corioles wear,
          And mothers that lack sons.

                    MENENIUS
          Now, the gods crown thee!

                    CORIOLANUS
                  (greets him warmly)
          And live you yet?

                    VOLUMNIA
                  (laughs)
          I know not where to turn. O, welcome
          home!
                    (MORE)

>   VOLUMNIA (cont'd)
>   And welcome, general. And you're welcome
>   all!
>
>   MENENIUS
>   A hundred thousand welcomes!

Coriolanus is surrounded by well-wishers and political
admirers. Volumnia and Menenius usher him along.

We see the image from TV: The noble warrior returned home.
Devoted family. Flags waving. The future golden.

24   INT. VILLA-BATHROOM - EVENING   24

And then the hard reality.

Coriolanus' body is a battleground of scars. Some are livid
and red, fresh and still oozing blood. Others are pale and
blue, discolored and dead.

His body is something monstrous. Stitched up. Patched
together. Slashed around. Frankenstein's monster.

He is leaning against a sink, stripped naked. His muscular if
shattered body exposed.

Volumnia sits and dresses her son's wounds. As she always has
done. As she always will.

It is a disturbing, intimate image.

>   CORIOLANUS
>   The good Senators must be visited;
>   From whom I have received not only
>   greetings,
>   But with them change of honors.

He shifts painfully as she continues to treat one of his
wounds.

>   VOLUMNIA
>   I have lived
>   To see inherited my very wishes
>   And the buildings of my fancy. Only
>   There's one thing wanting, which I doubt
>   not but
>   Our Rome will cast upon thee.

He catches her eye in the mirror, very firm:

                    CORIOLANUS
          Know, good mother,
          I had rather be their servant in my way,
          Than sway with them in theirs.

They stop when--

Virgilia enters.

She stops in the doorway. It is embarrassing for her, as if
she has interrupted two lovers. A long moment.

She looks to her husband.

To Volumnia.

They stare back.

There is no way she can compete with their intimacy.

Surrendering, she silently goes.

25   INT. VILLA -- HALLWAY - EVENING   25

Virgilia wanders a long hallway, past a fine collection of
antique Roman weaponry. She seems lost.

She stops and opens a door, glances into her son's bedroom:

Young Martius is asleep.

Her eyes move across his room. The military toys. The little
cadet uniform carefully hung. The polished boots waiting.

All stern and joyless. Not like a child's room at all.

Virgilia closes the door and continues down the long hallway,
disappearing into darkness.

26   INT. VILLA-BEDROOM - NIGHT   26

Coriolanus is on the bed. Staring up. Thinking.

Virgilia enters. She sits on the edge of the bed. Look at
him.

She reaches out. Touches his face.

He turns and looks at her.

27   INT. SENATE-CORRIDOR - DAY   27

Brutus and Sicinius hurry to the Senate chamber:

                    SICINIUS
          He cannot <u>temperately</u> transport his
          honors, but will
          Lose those he hath won.

                    BRUTUS
          I heard him swear,
          Were he to stand for Consul, never would
          he
          Appear in the marketplace nor
          Showing, as the manner is, his wounds
          To the people, beg "their stinking
          breaths."

                    SICINIUS
          It was his word.

They nod to some colleagues as they pass.

                    BRUTUS
          So it must fall out with him,
          Or <u>our</u> authorities at an end.

                    SICINIUS
          We must suggest to the people in what
          hatred
          He still hath held them.

                    BRUTUS
               (shushing him)
          Peace...

They enter the Senate Chamber...

28   INT. SENATE CHAMBER - DAY   28

Brutus and Sicinius make their way to their seats as we hear:

                    MENENIUS (V.O.)
          ... It remains,
          As the main point of this our after-
          meeting,
          To gratify his noble service that
          Hath thus stood for his country...

The interior of the grand Senate is an airy, sweeping chamber
that suggests the Israeli Knesset or U.N. General Assembly.

Again, classical symmetry is the rule with tiers of seats
facing a central dais. An imposing piece of outdated modern
art suggesting the might of Rome looms over the chamber like
a bird of prey.

Network TV cameras purr quietly from a corner.

Menenius, Cominius, Coriolanus and several other politicos
are seating at a central table on the dais, facing the rows
of SENATORS.

Menenius is standing at a podium, speaking into a microphone:

                    MENENIUS
          ... Therefore, please you,
          Most reverend and grave elders, to desire
          The present Consul, and last general
          In our well-found successes, to report
          A little of that worthy work performed
          By Caius Martius Coriolanus.

                    SENATOR
          Speak, good Cominius.

General Cominius rises and moves to the podium.

But then Coriolanus abruptly stands--

                    MENENIUS
          Nay, keep your place.

                    SENATOR
          Sit, Coriolanus. Never shame to hear
          What you have nobly done.

                    CORIOLANUS
          Your honors' pardon.
          I had rather have my wounds to heal again
          Than hear say how I got them.

                    MENENIUS
          Pray now, sit down.

                    CORIOLANUS
          I had rather have one scratch my head in
          the sun
          When the alarum were struck than idly sit
          To hear my nothings monstered.

Coriolanus moves across the dais and exits into a hallway.
The door shuts after him.

Menenius sighs. Nods to Cominius.

Cominius moves to the podium and begins to read his speech
from a Teleprompter. This all has the rehearsed quality of a
campaign nomination speech.

                    COMINIUS
          The deeds of Coriolanus
          Should not be uttered feebly. It is held
          That valor is the chiefest virtue, and
          Most dignifies the haver. <u>Alone</u> he
          entered
          The mortal gate of the city,
          And struck Corioles like a planet,
          From face to foot
          He was a thing of blood...

Brutus and Sicinius exchange a glance, bored by the political
boilerplate.

29   INT. SENATE-SERVICE CORRIDOR - DAY   29

Meanwhile, Coriolanus stands in the service corridor beyond
the chamber. Green industrial walls. Ugly fluorescent lights
above.

He leans against a wall, alone with his thoughts.

Cominius' voice can be heard droning inside.

Then Coriolanus glances up. A CUSTODIAN is pushing a garbage
can down the long corridor. He stops when he sees Coriolanus.

Coriolanus' cool, uncompromising stare makes the Custodian
uneasy. He turns around and goes back.

Coriolanus waits. His face strangely vacant.

He flexes his wounded arm. It hurts.

He hears Cominius finish. A good round of applause. He hears
his name being cheered: "Coriolanus!"

Coriolanus closes his eyes, steels himself, and then re-
enters the chamber...

30   INT. SENATE CHAMBER - DAY   30

... Menenius greets him and escorts him to the podium for his
"acceptance speech."

                    MENENIUS
        The Senate, Coriolanus, are well pleased
        To make thee Consul!

Menenius steps back.

A beat.

Coriolanus stares at the Senators. At the TV cameras.

He leans awkwardly into the podium microphone:

                  CORIOLANUS
        I do owe them still
        My life and services.

A beat.

For an acceptance speech, rather terse. Menenius jumps in to
salvage the moment:

                    MENENIUS
        It then remains
        That you do speak to the people.

                  CORIOLANUS
        I do beseech you,
        Let me overleap that custom, for I cannot
        entreat them
        For my wounds' sake to give their
        suffrage.
        Please you that I may pass this doing.

From the Senate floor, Sicinius jumps on this:

                    SICINIUS
        Sir, <u>the people</u>
        Must have their voices!

The Senators, led by Brutus, clamor their agreement.
Tradition must be obeyed.

                    MENENIUS
          (calming, to Coriolanus)
        Pray you, go fit you to the custom.

                  CORIOLANUS
        It is a part
        That I shall blush in acting, and might
        well
        Be taken from the people.

Menenius quickly turns off Coriolanus' microphone.

                    BRUTUS
                 (to Sicinius)
          Mark you that?

                    CORIOLANUS
          To brag unto them "Thus I did, and thus!"
          Show them the unaching scars which I
          should hide,
          As if I had received them for the hire
          Of their breath only!

Menenius sees Coriolanus is getting angry, this could be
disastrous.

He elegantly gestures for Cominius to escort Coriolanus out
immediately -- as he addresses the Senators and TV cameras:

                    MENENIUS
          To our noble Consul
          Wish we all joy and honor!

He applauds. The applause is taken up by the Senators. Some
cheering as well for the hero of Rome ... The two Tribunes,
however, are already whispering maliciously to other
Senators.

Menenius seems pleased with the general response. So far, so
good.

31   INT. VILLA -- LIVING ROOM - DAY   31

Volumnia is pleased as well.

She sits, watching the events unfold on TV.

The sound of the cheering fades as we go to...

32   INT. MENENIUS' LIMO - DAY   32

The limousine winds through the pedestrian traffic toward the
Roman marketplace.

Coriolanus sits with Menenius. Coriolanus is both angry and
embarrassed. He is wearing a sharp business suit.

                    MENENIUS
          Have you not known
          The worthiest men have done it?

                         CORIOLANUS
                    (agrees)
          Custom calls me to it.
          What custom wills, in all things should
          we do...
          What must I say?
          "Look, sir, my wounds.
          I got them in my country's service."

                         MENENIUS
          O me, the gods!
          You must not speak like that. You must
          desire them
          To think upon you--

                         CORIOLANUS
          "Think upon me"? Hang 'em!
          I would they would forget me.

                         MENENIUS
          You'll mar all!

The limo stops. They are at the marketplace. The moment has
come.

Menenius takes a breath. Urges calm:

                         MENENIUS
          Pray you, speak to them, I pray you,
          In wholesome manner.

                         CORIOLANUS
                    (sourly)
          Bid them wash their faces
          And keep their teeth clean.

He leaves the car.

33   EXT. MARKETPLACE - DAY   33

The commercial heart of Rome. A large town square, since
antiquity used as a marketplace.

But now it is filled with tatty stalls selling cheap purses
and knock-off watches. Paltry fruit stands alongside shabby
souvenir stalls.

Advertising billboards surround and pollute the square   --
SONY. COKE. NIKE. MCDONALDS -- obscuring any classical
architecture that might have survived.

Tamora and Cassius, the political activists, are in the crowd. They watch closely.

Coriolanus slowly walks into the marketplace. He has armed security with him.

He walks to the center of the market. He stands, feeling ridiculous and not at all humble.

He looks around.

Waiting for something to happen.

The CUSTOMERS and SHOPKEEPERS just look back at him. Some are curious. Some are amused. Some hostile and most indifferent.

But no one approaches.

Then Coriolanus understands. He must go to them: beg for votes.

He prepares himself and then slowly moves through the various stalls, weaving in and out. Trying to maintain his dignity.

He sees the Citizens from before and goes to them. We glimpse Brutus and Sicinius amongst the crowd.

                    CORIOLANUS
               (to Cassius)
          You know the cause, sir, of my standing
          here.

                    CASSIUS
          We do, sir. Tell us what hath brought you
          to it.

                    CORIOLANUS
          Mine own desert.

                    TAMORA
          Your own desert?

                    CORIOLANUS
          Ay, but not mine own desire.

                    TAMORA
          How not your own desire?

                    CORIOLANUS
          No, it was never my desire yet to trouble
          the poor with begging.

                    CASSIUS
        You must think, if we give you anything,
        we hope to gain by you.

                    CORIOLANUS
        Well then, I pray, your price of the
        Consulship?

                    WAR VET
        The price is to ask it kindly.

                    CORIOLANUS
        Kindly, sir, I pray, let me have it. I
        have wounds to show you, which shall be
        yours in private ... Your good voice,
        sir. What say you?

                    WAR VET
                 (impressed)
        You shall have it, worthy sir.

                    CORIOLANUS
        A match, sir. There's in all two worthy
        voices begged. I have your alms. Adieu.

Business done, so he thinks, Coriolanus crisply moves on.

Cassius is not convinced.

                    CASSIUS
        But this is something odd.

Coriolanus continues on. He sees a large JAMAICAN WOMAN with
her CHILDREN, carrying plastic grocery bags, talking to a
SHOPKEEPER. He goes to them:

                    CORIOLANUS
        Pray you now, if it may stand with the
        tune of your voices that I may be Consul.

                    JAMAICAN WOMAN
        You have deserved nobly of your country,
        and you have not deserved nobly.

                    CORIOLANUS
        Your enigma?

                    JAMAICAN WOMAN
        You have been a scourge to her enemies;
        you have been a rod to her friends ...
        You have not indeed loved the common
        people.

                    CORIOLANUS
You should account me the more virtuous
that I have not been common in my love
... Therefore, beseech you, I may be
Consul.

                    SHOPKEEPER
We hope to find you our friend, and
therefore give you our voices heartily.

                    JAMAICAN WOMAN
You have received many wounds for your
country.

                    CORIOLANUS
I will not seal your knowledge with
showing them. I will make much of your
voices, and so trouble you no farther.

                    JAMAICAN WOMAN
The gods give you joy, sir, heartily!

Coriolanus is warming to the task, it's easier than he
thought. He moves to a central, open area and declares
publicly:

                    CORIOLANUS
Your voices! For your voices I have
fought;
Watched for your voices; for your voices
bear
Of wounds two dozen odd; battles thrice
six
I have seen and heard of!

A crowd is gathering. We note Brutus and Sicinius in the
crowd. Menenius, too, has moved in.

                    CORIOLANUS
For your voices
Have done many things, some less, some
more.
Your voices! Indeed, I would be Consul.

                    WAR VET
He has done nobly, and cannot go without
any honest man's voice!

                    RACE TRACK TOUT
Therefore let him be Consul!

                    JAMAICAN WOMAN
          The gods give him joy, and make him good
          friend to the people!

The Citizens applaud and give their support:

                       CITIZENS
          Amen, amen. God save thee, noble Consul!

                      CORIOLANUS
          Worthy voices!

Menenius, with Brutus and Sicinius, goes to him:

                       MENENIUS
          You have stood your limitation, and the
          Tribunes
          Endue you with the people's voice.

                      CORIOLANUS
          Is this done?

                       SICINIUS
          The custom of request you have
          discharged.
          The people do admit you, and are summoned
          To meet anon upon your approbation.

                      CORIOLANUS
          Where? At the Senate?

                       SICINIUS
          There, Coriolanus.

                       MENENIUS
          I'll keep you company.
                (to Brutus)
          Will you along?

                        BRUTUS
                (declines)
          We stay here for the people.

Coriolanus and Menenius go, relieved the trial is over.

Brutus and Sicinius, however, have work to do. This has not
gone as they wanted. They are urgent:

                       SICINIUS
          How now, my masters! Have you chose this
          man?

                    CASSIUS
               (ruefully)
          He has our voices, sir.

                    BRUTUS
          We pray the gods he may deserve your
          loves.

                    TAMORA
          Amen, sir. To my poor unworthy notice,
          He mocked us when he begged our voices.

                    CASSIUS
          Certainly
          He flouted us downright.

                    JAMAICAN WOMAN
          No, it is his kind of speech; he did not
          mock us.

                    TAMORA
               (sharply)
          He should have showed us
          His marks of merit, wounds received for's
          country.

                    SICINIUS
          Why, so he did, I am sure.

                    TAMORA
          No, no! No one saw them!

                    CASSIUS
               (inciting the crowd)
          Was not this mockery?

Brutus presses hard:

                    BRUTUS
          When he had no power,
          But was a petty servant to the state,
          He was your enemy, ever spake against
          Your liberties.

                    SICINIUS
          Did you perceive
          He did solicit you in free contempt
          When he did need your loves, and do you
          think
          That his contempt shall not be bruising
          to you
          When he hath power to crush?

Cassius and Tamora carefully lead the crowd in expressing
growing alarm and resistance to Coriolanus:

> CASSIUS
> He's not confirmed; we may deny him yet!

> TAMORA
> And will deny him!
> I'll have five hundred voices of that
> sound.

> CASSIUS
> I twice five hundred and their friends!

The crowd roars approval. A frightening, animal sound.

> SICINIUS
> Let them assemble,
> And on a safer judgment all revoke
> Your ignorant election.

> BRUTUS
> Enforce his pride,
> And his old hate unto you!

> SICINIUS
> And presently, when you have drawn your
> number,
> Repair to the Capitol.

> CASSIUS
> We will so!

> TAMORA
> We will so! All
> Repent in their election!

Cassius and Tamora lead the crowd. It is a terrifying
spectacle of sudden mob rage, only a razor-thin edge to
violence.

Brutus and Sicinius watch, satisfied, like Robespierre and
Saint Just looking over the bloody guillotine.

34   INT. SENATE-ANTECHAMBER - DAY   34

Coriolanus is putting on his familiar uniform.

Menenius, General Cominius, and several pro-Coriolanus
Senators are with him.

Martius is having a video conference with his comrade Titus.
Titus is in the field, wearing combat gear.

                    CORIOLANUS
                (to Titus)
          Tullus Aufidius then has assembled a new
          army?

                    TITUS
                (on screen)
          He has, my lord.

                    CORIOLANUS
          Saw you Aufidius?

                    TITUS
                (on screen)
          He is retired to Antium.

                    CORIOLANUS
          Spoke he of me?

                    TITUS
                (on screen)
          He did, my lord.

                    CORIOLANUS
          How? What?

                    TITUS
                (on screen)
          How often he had met you, sword to sword;
          That of all things upon the earth he
          hated
          Your person most.

                    CORIOLANUS
          At Antium lives he?

                    TITUS
                (on screen)
          At Antium.

Menenius is beckoning for Coriolanus to go. They're late.

                    CORIOLANUS
          I wish I had a cause to seek him there,
          To oppose his hatred fully.

He ends the computer link to Titus and they leave the
antechamber...

35   INT. SENATE-CENTRAL LOBBY - DAY   35

The central lobby of the Senate is an open, airy space.

Through the glass doors at the front of the lobby an unruly
crowd can be seen gathering. Police. Barricades.

Sicinius and Brutus are waiting to intercept them.

                    CORIOLANUS
          Behold, these are the Tribunes of the
          people,
          The tongues of the common mouth.

                    SICINIUS
          Pass no further.

                    CORIOLANUS
          Ha! What is that?

                    BRUTUS
          It will be dangerous to go on. No
          further.

                    CORIOLANUS
          What makes this change?

                    MENENIUS
          The matter?

                    COMINIUS
          Hath he not passed the nobles and the
          commons?

                    BRUTUS
          Cominius, no.

Coriolanus steps closer to Brutus. The mob sees him through
the glass doors. The tension immediately increases.

                    CORIOLANUS
          Have I had children's voices?

                    MENENIUS
          Tribunes, give way.

                    BRUTUS
          The people are incensed against him.

                    CORIOLANUS
                (glancing to the growing
                crowd)
        Are these your herd?

                    MENENIUS
        Be calm, be calm.

                    BRUTUS
        The people cry you <u>mocked</u> <u>them</u>, and of
        late called them
        Time-pleasers, flatterers, foes to
        nobleness.

                    CORIOLANUS
        But this was known before.

                    SICINIUS
        You show too much of that
        For which the people stir. If you will
        pass
        To where you are bound, you must inquire
        your way.

The crowd outside is growing restless, sensing and responding
to the building tension. The police try to hold them back,
keeping them away from the doors. The crowd presses in.

We see Cassius and Tamora at the forefront, urging the crowd
on.

                    MENENIUS
        Let's be calm--

                    COMINIUS
        The people are abused, set on--

                    MENENIUS
        Not now, not now--

                    COMINIUS
        Not in this heat, sir--

Coriolanus refers viciously to the crowd outside:

                    CORIOLANUS
        My nobler friends, I crave their pardons.
        For the mutable, rank-scented crowd,
        Let them regard me as I do not flatter,
        And therein behold themselves. I say
        again,
        In soothing them, we nourish against our
        Senate
                    (MORE)

                    CORIOLANUS (cont'd)
The cockle of <u>rebellion</u>, <u>insolence</u>,
<u>sedition</u>,
Which we ourselves have ploughed for,
sowed, and scattered,
By mingling <u>them</u> with <u>us</u>!

                    MENENIUS
Well, no more!

                    COMINIUS
No more words, we beseech you--

                    BRUTUS
          (to Coriolanus, provoking)
You speak of the people
As if you were a god to punish, not
A man of their infirmity.

                    SICINIUS
It were well we let the people know it.

                    CORIOLANUS
Were I as patient as the midnight sleep,
By Jove, it would be my mind!

                    SICINIUS
It is a mind
That shall remain a poison where it is,
Not poison any further.

                    CORIOLANUS
          (explodes)
"<u>Shall</u> <u>remain</u>"!
Hear you this Triton of the minnows? Mark
you
His absolute "shall"?

                    BRUTUS
Why, should the people give
One that speaks thus their voice?

                    CORIOLANUS
I'll give my reasons,
More worthier than their voices!

Menenius tries to pull him away, Coriolanus shakes free and
continues the attack:

                    CORIOLANUS
By Jove himself,
It makes the consuls base; and my soul
aches
To know, when two authorities are up,
Neither supreme, how soon confusion,
          (MORE)

>   CORIOLANUS (cont'd)
>   May enter 'twixt the gap of both and take
>   The one by the other.

The crowd roars angrily outside -- Coriolanus spins on them:

>   CORIOLANUS
>   Thus we debase the nature of our seats,
>   and make the rabble
>   Call our cares fears; which will in time
>   Break ope the locks of the Senate, and
>   bring in
>   The crows to peck the eagles!

>   MENENIUS
>   Come, enough!

>   BRUTUS
>   Enough, with over-measure.

>   SICINIUS
>   He has spoken like a traitor, and shall
>   answer
>   As traitors do!

At the word "traitor" Coriolanus loses all reason, he is
fire:

>   CORIOLANUS
>   Thou wretch, despite overwhelm thee!

>   BRUTUS
>   Manifest treason!

>   SICINIUS
>   This is a Consul? No!

>   CORIOLANUS
>   Hence, old goat!

Coriolanus grabs Sicinius roughly and shoves him through the
doors to the outside--

36   EXT. SENATE-COURTYARD - DAY   36

Coriolanus flings Sicinius aside--

The others spill outside--

The crowd ROARS in outrage--

Menenius pulls Coriolanus off:

> MENENIUS
> On both sides more respect!

> SICINIUS
> (calling to the crowd)
> Here's he that would take from you all
> your power!

The mob has surrounded them all by now. This all has the potential of sparking to violence.

We note TV news crews hustling for position, covering the action. Others film with cell phone cameras. *We intercut some of this footage.*

We see grim RIOT POLICE marching into position. The crowd is not intimidated, they are spoiling for a fight.

The Tribunes provoke the crowd even more, escalating and building the fever:

> BRUTUS
> You are at point to lose your liberties!
> Martius would have all from you, Martius,
> Whom late you have named for Consul.

> SICINIUS
> What is the city but the people?!

> TAMORA
> True! The people are the city!

> SICINIUS
> We do here pronounce, upon the part of
> the people,
> Martius is worthy of present <u>DEATH</u>!

A huge roar from the mob. Panic and violence building. Fast and overlapping:

> BRUTUS
> Guards, seize him!

> CORIOLANUS
> No, I'll die here!

> BRUTUS
> Lay hands upon him!

> SICINIUS
> (to the crowd)
> HELP, YE CITIZENS!

At his cue--

The civil violence threatened from the opening moments of
this story finally EXPLODES--

With Cassius and Tamora in the forefront, the crowd attacks
the police--

Riot Police march in, slamming ahead with riot shields and
truncheons--

The mob fights back with anything at hand -- some are armed
with clubs and knives, others snatch up garbage cans and
newspaper vending machines, throwing them, smashing windows,
battling the police, kicking and punching and screaming--

It is civil disobedience. But it is also drunken, thug
violence. Terrifying in its intensity--

Menenius and Cominius hustle Coriolanus away--

> MENENIUS
> Go, get you to your house! Be gone, away!
> All will be naught else--

> COMINIUS
> Come, sir, along with us--

They hurry Coriolanus away--

The Riot Police, outnumbered, start firing TEAR GAS into the
crowd--

Screams--

TV news crew filming--

Chaotic, flurried violence--

Shaky TV images, cell phone video--

Choking, acrid gas--

It is a terrifying descent into public madness as all order
breaks down.

Rome is bloody.

37   INT. SENATE-OFFICE - DUSK   37

Menenius and the Tribunes are gathered in a darkened office
for some high-stakes politicking.

Tamora, her face bloody from the riot, is with them. So too some supporters on either side.

                    MENENIUS
               (urgently)
          As I do know the Consul's worthiness,
          So can I name his faults--

                    SICINIUS
          Consul! What Consul?

                    MENENIUS
          The Consul Coriolanus.

                    BRUTUS
          He Consul?!

                    SICINIUS
          It is decreed
          He dies tonight.

                    TAMORA
          He's a disease that must be cut away.

                    MENENIUS
          O, he's a limb that has but a disease:
          Mortal, to cut it off; to cure it, easy.
          What has he done to Rome that's worth his
          death? Eh?
          Killing our enemies?!

He sees that his words are having some effect, he presses the point:

                    MENENIUS
          The blood he hath lost --
          He dropped it _for_ _his_ _country_.

Some in the room murmur agreement.

                    BRUTUS
          We'll hear no more--

                    MENENIUS
          Consider this: he has been bred in the
          wars
          Since he could draw a sword, and is ill
          schooled
          In graceful language ... Give me leave,
          I'll go to him, and undertake to bring
          him
          Where he shall answer by a lawful form,
          In peace, to his utmost peril.

                    PRO-CORIOLANUS SENATOR
          Noble tribunes,
          It is the humane way.

                    ANOTHER SENATOR
          The other course
          Will prove too bloody, and the end of it
          Unknown to the beginning.

Sicinius is about to retort when Brutus stops him.

Brutus assents, assuming the voice of reason:

                    BRUTUS
          Be you then as the people's officer.

Menenius and Coriolanus' supporters are relieved.

                    BRUTUS
          If you bring not Martius, we'll proceed
          In our first way.

                    MENENIUS
          I'll bring him to you.

He goes quickly.

Brutus turns to Sicinius and Tamora and begins to quietly
explain his plan.

38 INT. MARTIUS VILLA-CORRIDOR - DAY   38

Coriolanus strides angrily down a long corridor, in and out
of shafts of light, seething to Virgilia:

                    CORIOLANUS
          Let them pull all about mine ears,
          present me
          Death on the wheel or at wild horses'
          heels,
          Yet will I still be thus to them--!

                    VIRGILIA
          Martius--

                    CORIOLANUS
                (continuing unabated)
          I muse my mother
          Does not approve me further!

He slams through a door to the living room...

39   INT. VILLA -- LIVING ROOM - DAY   39

... And stomps to confront his mother, who is currently
conspiring with Menenius, Cominius and a few Senators.

                    CORIOLANUS
                (to Volumnia, angrily)
          I talk of you!
          Why did you wish me milder? Would you
          have me
          False to my nature? Rather say I play
          The man I am!

She is equally tough with him, not giving an inch, snapping
right back:

                    VOLUMNIA
          O, sir, sir, sir,
          I would have had you put your power well
          on,
          Before you had worn it out.

                    CORIOLANUS
          Let go!

                    VOLUMNIA
          You might have been enough the man you
          are,
          With striving less to be so!

                    CORIOLANUS
          Let them hang!

                    VOLUMNIA
          Ay, and burn too!

Her outraged fury matches his. Overpowers his.

                    MENENIUS
                (to Coriolanus)
          Come, come, you have been too rough,
          something too rough.
          You must return and mend it.

Coriolanus turns away.

                    VOLUMNIA
          Pray, be counseled.
          I have a heart as little apt as yours,
          But yet a brain that leads my use of
          anger
          To better vantage.

                        MENENIUS
          Well said, noble woman!

                        CORIOLANUS
          What must I do?

                        MENENIUS
          Return to the Tribunes.

                        CORIOLANUS
          Well, what then? What then?

                        MENENIUS
          Repent what you have spoke.

                        CORIOLANUS
          For them? I cannot do it to the gods.
          Must I then do it to them?

                        VOLUMNIA
          You are too absolute,
          Though therein you can never be too
          noble.

                        CORIOLANUS
                  (upset, walking away)
          Why force you this?

She pursues him:

                        VOLUMNIA
          Because that now it lies you on to speak
          To the people, not by your own
          instruction,
          Nor by the matter which your heart
          prompts you,
          But with such words that are but
          rehearsed in
          Your tongue, though but bastards and
          syllables
          Of no allowance to your bosom's truth...

She moves closer to him. Her voice lower. A sort of
seduction.

                        VOLUMNIA
          I would dissemble with my nature where
          My fortunes and my friends at stake
          required
          I should do so in honor...

She is very close now. Whispering. She touches him gently,
like a lover.

                    VOLUMNIA
          I am in this your wife, your son,
          These senators, the nobles ...
          And you.

A long beat. All are silent, watching her spin her web.

                    VOLUMNIA
          I prithee now, my son,
          Go and say to them
          Thou art their <u>soldier</u>, and being bred in
          broils
          Has not the soft way
          In asking their good loves; but thou wilt
          frame
          Thyself, forsooth, hereafter <u>theirs</u>.

                    MENENIUS
          This but done, even as she speaks,
          Why their hearts were yours.

                    VOLUMNIA
          Prithee now,
          Go, and be ruled...
                    (laughing to him)
          Although I know thou hadst rather
          Follow thine enemy in a fiery gulf
          Than flatter him in a bower.

Coriolanus smiles. A genuinely sweet moment between them.

                    COMINIUS
          Sir, it is fit
          You make strong party, or defend yourself
          By calmness or by absence. All's in
          anger.

                    MENENIUS
          Only fair speech.

                    COMINIUS
          I think it will serve, if he
          Can thereto frame his spirit.

                    VOLUMNIA
          He must -- <u>and</u> <u>will</u>.
                    (to Coriolanus)
          Prithee now, say you will, and go about
          it.

                    CORIOLANUS
          Must I
          With base tongue give my noble heart
                    (MORE)

>   CORIOLANUS (cont'd)
>   A lie that it must bear? ... Well, I will
>   do it.

But he is still agitated. Volumnia shares a concerned glance with Menenius.

>   CORIOLANUS
>   (bitterly)
>   Away, my disposition, and possess me
>   Some harlot's spirit. A beggar's tongue
>   Make motion through my lips.

The thought of begging is too much, he rejects it, breaking away:

>   CORIOLANUS
>   I will not do it!
>   Lest I cease to honor mine own truth
>   And by my body's action teach my mind
>   A most inherent baseness.

Volumnia snarls at him, exasperated, building to a thunder that dwarfs his:

>   VOLUMNIA
>   At thy choice, then!
>   To beg of thee, it is my more dishonor
>   Than thou of them. Come all to ruin! Let
>   Thy mother rather feel thy pride than
>   fear
>   Thy dangerous stoutness, for I mock at
>   death
>   With as big heart as thou! Do as you
>   like!

The words echo.

It is as if he has been slapped. His resolve vanishes.

>   CORIOLANUS
>   Pray, be content...
>   Mother, I am going, chide me no more.

He awaits her approval.

She will not yet grant it.

>   CORIOLANUS
>   Look, I am going...
>   (a glance to Virgilia)
>   I'll return Consul,
>   Or never trust to what my tongue can do
>   In the way of flattery further.

Volumnia graciously bows to him.

>   VOLUMNIA
>   Do your will.

Then she kisses him.

And she goes.

Like a queen. Volumnia triumphant. Always.

Then a shocking hard cut to:

40   INT. TELEVISION STUDIO - DAY   40

A crowded TV studio. The audience stands are filling up.
Television cameras. Lights. Heavy security.

On the stage: the set for a chat show. Translight of a city
skyline behind the set. Two standing microphones.

At the side of the set, Sicinius and Brutus are conspiring
with the two citizen activists, Cassius and Tamora:

>   BRUTUS
>   (to Sicinius)
>   In this point charge him home: that he
>   affects
>   Tyrannical power. If he evade us there,
>   Enforce him with his envy to the people.

>   SICINIUS
>   (to Tamora)
>   Have you a catalogue
>   Of all the voices that we have procured
>   Set down by the poll?

>   TAMORA
>   I have; it's ready.

>   SICINIUS
>   When the people hear me say "It shall be
>   so
>   In the right and strength of the
>   Commons," be it either
>   For death, for fine, or banishment, then
>   let them,
>   If I say "Fine," cry "Fine!" - if
>   "Death," cry "Death!"

>   TAMORA
>   We shall inform them.

Cassius and Tamora hurry off to instruct and manipulate the crowd as best they can. They mix with the audience in the stands.

Meanwhile--

A gloomy but resolved Coriolanus walks with Cominius and Menenius between the tiers of audience, on the way to the set.

> COMINIUS
> Arm yourself
> To answer <u>mildly</u>, for they are prepared
> With accusations, as I hear, more strong
> Than are upon you yet.

> CORIOLANUS
> The word is "mildly." Pray you, let us go.
> Let them accuse me by invention, I
> Will answer in mine honor.

> MENENIUS
> Ay, but mildly.

> CORIOLANUS
> Well, mildly be it then. Mildly!

Coriolanus steels himself as they emerge from between the stands and head toward the set.

TV news crews are waiting. Blinding lights snap on.

The crowd, on seeing Coriolanus, lets out a ROAR. Deafening and savage.

We see Cassius and Tamora moving through the crowd, instigating, convincing, imploring.

Coriolanus ignores it all.

Brutus and Sicinius wait on the set.

> BRUTUS
> (whispers to Sicinius)
> Put him to choler straight.

Coriolanus and his supporters move to the stage. Coriolanus glares at the Tribunes. The TV crews take up position.

Menenius gestures for Coriolanus to step to the microphone, whispering to him:

                        MENENIUS
              <u>Calmly</u>, I do beseech you.

Coriolanus steps to the microphone.

Brutus gestures for the crowd to quiet down.

We see bits of this scene through the monitors on the TV
cameras.

When the crowd is silent, Coriolanus begins to make a
rehearsed speech:

                        CORIOLANUS
              The honored gods--

But his voice echoes badly with reverb. Menenius adjusts the
microphone. Coriolanus begins again, quickly and by rote:

                        CORIOLANUS
              The honored gods
              Keep Rome in safety, and the chairs of
              justice
              Supplied with worthy men. Plant love
              among us.
              Throng our large temples with the shows
              of peace,
              And not our streets with war.

                        COMINIUS
              Amen, amen.

                        MENENIUS
              A noble wish.

His boilerplate speech over, Coriolanus turns to Sicinius who
is at the other standing microphone:

                        CORIOLANUS
              Shall I be charged no further than this
              present?
              Must all determine here?

                        SICINIUS
              I do demand,
              If you submit you to the people's voices.

                        CORIOLANUS
              I am content.

41   INT. VILLA -- LIVING ROOM - DAY   41

Volumnia watches the proceedings closely on TV. She is
pleased with her son's performance so far.

42   INT. TELEVISION STUDIO - DAY   42

Menenius, ever the People's Friend, steps to the microphone:

>   MENENIUS
>   Lo, citizens, he says he is content.
>   The warlike service he has done,
>   consider; think
>   Upon the <u>wounds</u> his body bears, which
>   show
>   Like graves in the holy churchyard.
>
>   CORIOLANUS
>   (uncomfortable with this)
>   Scratches with briers,
>   Scars to move laughter only.

43   INT. APARTMENT - DAY   43

Aufidius sits with several of his officers, leaning forward,
watching the drama unfold on TV.

44   INT. TELEVISION STUDIO - DAY   44

>   MENENIUS
>   Consider further,
>   That when he speaks not like a citizen,
>   You find him like a <u>soldier</u>. Do not take
>   His rougher accents for malicious sounds,
>   But, as I say, such as become a soldier.

Coriolanus cuts in, his impatience getting the better of him:

>   CORIOLANUS
>   What is the matter
>   That being passed for Consul with full
>   voice,
>   I am so dishonored that the very hour
>   You take it off again?
>
>   SICINIUS
>   We charge you that you have contrived to
>   take
>   From Rome all seasoned office, and to
>   (MORE)

                    SICINIUS (cont'd)
wind
Yourself into a power tyrannical ...
          (the coup de grace)
For which you are a <u>traitor</u> to the
people.

Coriolanus responds, a cobra striking:

                    CORIOLANUS
How? <u>Traitor</u>?!

                    MENENIUS
          (alarmed)
Nay, temperately! Your promise.

                    CORIOLANUS
The fires in the lowest hell fold in the
people!
Call me their <u>traitor</u>, thou injurious
Tribune!

                    SICINIUS
          (calling)
Mark you this, people?!

The crowd responds, egged on by Cassius and Tamora. A murmur
of voices, a chant growing, "Traitor ... traitor ...
traitor..."

Brutus cleverly plays the reasonable voice, knowing his words
will further rile Coriolanus:

                    BRUTUS
But since he hath
Served well for Rome--

                    CORIOLANUS
          (snaps)
What do you prate of service?

                    BRUTUS
I talk of that, that know it.

                    CORIOLANUS
You?! ...
I'll know no further.
Let them pronounce death, exile,
Flaying, pent to linger
But with a grain a day - I would not buy
Their mercy at the price of one fair
word!

45   INT. VILLA -- LIVING ROOM - DAY   45

Volumnia watches, alarmed now. She knows this rage could
prove to be disastrous for her son.

46   INT. TELEVISION STUDIO - DAY   46

Sicinius seizes the moment to destroy Coriolanus, barking
into the microphone:

                    SICINIUS
          In the name of the people
          And in the power of us the Tribunes, we,
          Even from this instant, <u>banish</u> him our
          city!
          In the people's name,
          I say ... IT SHALL BE SO!

Well-rehearsed by Cassius and Tamora, many in the crowd
respond with a fierce cry:

                    CROWD
          It shall be so! It shall be so!

                    TAMORA
          He's banished! IT SHALL BE SO!

                    CROWD
          It shall be so! It shall be so! It shall
          be so...!

Cassius and Tamora keep the crowd at a fever pitch--

They keep chanting and railing--

A building seismic rumble--

                    COMINIUS
               (stepping forward)
          Hear me, my masters, and my common
          friends--!

                    SICINIUS
          He's sentenced. No more hearing.

                    COMINIUS
          Let me speak!

The crowd's fury is building--

It is all about to erupt--

                         BRUTUS
          There's no more to be said, but he is
          banished
          As enemy to the people and his country.
          IT SHALL BE SO!

                         CROWD
          It shall be so! It shall be so! It shall
          be so...!

And then--

Coriolanus explodes--

His rage is volcanic--

He SLAMS the standing microphone away--

His dragon's ROAR silences the entire studio--

                         CORIOLANUS
               YOU COMMON CRY OF CURS!

A collective intake of breath--

The crowd is stunned--

                         CORIOLANUS
          Whose breath I hate
          As reek of the rotten fens, whose loves I
          prize
          As the dead carcasses of unburied men
          That do corrupt my air...
                    (each word an attack)
          I ... BANISH ... YOU!

The crowd is silent. No one dares to even breathe.

AT THE VILLA: Volumnia watches, frozen, breathless.

IN THE APARTMENT: Aufidius stands, riveted.

BACK IN THE STUDIO:

                         CORIOLANUS
          Here remain with your uncertainty.
          Let every feeble rumor shake your hearts!
          Your enemies, with nodding of their
          plumes,
          Fan you into despair! Have the power
          still
          To banish your defenders, till at length
          Your ignorance - which finds not till it
                         (MORE)

                  CORIOLANUS (cont'd)
feels,
Making but reservation of yourselves;
Still your own foes - deliver you
As most abated captives to some nation
That won you without blows!

A beat.

The TV cameras hum. The crowd is silent.

Menenius and the others watch in amazement.

Coriolanus slowly takes one last, long look at the people of
Rome.

Then:

                  CORIOLANUS
Despising,
For you, the city, thus I turn my back.

He turns and slowly walks toward one of the tunnels leading
from the studio.

The crowd follows every step with their eyes.

He stops.

Turns back.

Steel.

                  CORIOLANUS
      There is a world elsewhere.

And he goes down the tunnel.

Disappearing from view.

A silent beat.

Then, a chilling cry of absolutely Jacobin bloodlust from the
stands:

                  TAMORA
    The people's enemy is gone!

The crowd SCREAMS their approval.

The SAVAGE CRY echoes around the studio.

The echoing roar takes us to...

47   EXT. WASTELAND CHECKPOINT - DAWN   47

The outskirts of Rome are an urban wasteland. Abandoned
factories. Rusting cars. Overgrown vacant lots. Collapsing
advertising billboards.

There is a lonely gas station in the distance, its neon sign
glowing a lurid green in the gray dawn light.

We are at a Roman checkpoint on the highway into the city. A
guardhouse and barrier. Some barbed wire barricades. Bored
soldiers.

Coriolanus slogs along the highway. Backpack slung over this
shoulder.

A certain darkness creeps in his expression. An ominous
resolve.

                    CORIOLANUS (V.O.)
               You shall hear from me still.

Miles and miles of wasteland and desolation ahead.

His future.

                    CORIOLANUS (V.O.)
               I go alone,
               Like to a lonely dragon.

The only sound is the cold, lonely moan of the wind.

We fade to...

48   EXT./INT. EXILE SEQUENCE - DAY/NIGHT   48

Coriolanus' exile.

We see his long odyssey. It is a grueling physical journey --
and also something of a spiritual challenge. He is solitary
and without comfort: vulnerable to the elements and also to
the demons of his own psyche.

We see him as...

He walks along the barren highway. Trash piled along the
road. A car zooms past. Whoosh. He is lost in dust...

Blazing heat, like a furnace, as he trudges over desert
terrain. Burning oil wells blacken the sky in the distance...

Isolated, within himself, as he walks past the detritus of war ... a burned out tank ... a mountain of rusted artillery shells ... skeletons bleached in the sun...

His clothes are dusty and dirty now. A sandstorm. He wraps a scarf around his head, like a burnoose. Only his eyes visible now...

A gypsy boy in tattered clothing riding a white horse passes him. The boy looks at him intently as he passes...

We get a sense of him moving into different terrain, up into a mountain range, climbing...

Then descending. Pouring rain. Lightning sparking. He is almost a Romantic figure now. Byronic. Wrapped in a cloak against the wildness of nature; the chiaroscuro flashes of light illuminating his haunted eyes...

We end at...

49   EXT. OUTSIDE ANTIUM - NIGHT   49

Coriolanus stands. Like a statue. All his life in his blazing eyes. He is staring at a small town in the distance.

We see a sign: ANTIUM.

His destination since he began. The home of his nemesis, the hated Aufidius.

He begins to walk to the town.

50   INT. POLITICO BAR - DAY   50

Meanwhile, back in Rome, Brutus and Sicinius are having lunch at their usual hangout.

They see Volumnia entering the restaurant, pulling Virgilia after her. An ambush. She heads toward the Tribunes.

Volumnia's eyes have the grim intensity of a predator. She looks strangely wild.

                    BRUTUS
          Here comes his mother.

                    SICINIUS
              (prepares to go)
          Let's not meet her. They say she's mad.

Volumnia stalks up to them:

>   VOLUMNIA
> O, you're well met. The hoarded plague of
> the gods
> Requite your love!

The Tribunes try to leave, she won't let them:

>   VOLUMNIA
> Will you be gone?

>   VIRGILIA
> You shall stay too. I would I had the
> power
> To say so to my husband.

>   SICINIUS
> Are you mad?

>   VOLUMNIA
> Ay, fool, is that a shame? Note but this,
> fool:
> Hadst thou craft
> To banish him that struck more blows for
> Rome
> Than thou hast spoken words?

>   SICINIUS
>   (trying to escape)
> O blessed heavens...

Volumnia is creating a scene. Heads are turning.

She continues her attack on Sicinius, but is distracted and
jumbled:

>   VOLUMNIA
> More noble blows than ever thou wise
> words,
> And for Rome's good. I'll tell thee what -
> Yet go--
> Nay -- but thou shalt stay too -- I would
> my son
> Were in Arabia, and thy tribe before him,
> His good sword in his hand.

>   SICINIUS
> What then?

>   VIRGILIA
> What then?
> He'd make an end of thy posterity.

                    VOLUMNIA
       Bastards <u>and</u> <u>all</u>.

Menenius has entered the bar, seeing the trouble he goes to
them, tries to calm Volumnia:

                    MENENIUS
       Come, come, peace...

                    BRUTUS
       Pray, let us go.

He tries to leave the bar. Volumnia stops him for final
attack, something like a curse in its power:

                    VOLUMNIA
       Now, pray, sir, get you gone.
       You have done a brave deed. Ere you go,
       hear this:
              (grabs Virgilia)
       This lady's husband here, this, do you
       see?!--
       Whom you have banished, does exceed you
       all.

                    BRUTUS
       Well, well, we'll leave you.

                    SICINIUS
       Why stay we to be baited
       With one that wants her wits?

                    VOLUMNIA
       I would the gods had nothing else to do
       But to confirm my curses!

Menenius gently restrains Volumnia and the Tribunes finally
escape the bar.

Volumnia takes a breath, controls herself.

                    VOLUMNIA
       Could I meet 'em
       But once a day, it would unclog my heart
       Of what lies heavy to it.

                    MENENIUS
       You have told them home;
       And, by my troth, you have cause. You'll
       sup with me?

She turns to him. A cold and killing fire in her eyes.

>   VOLUMNIA
>   Anger's my meat. I sup upon myself,
>   And so shall starve with feeding.

She takes Virgilia's hand and drags her out.

Menenius watches. Saddened.

Once proud Volumnia, reduced to this.

51   EXT. ANTIUM - NIGHT   51

Antium is an old Volscian city gone to seed. It is Latin in flavor, something like Havana.

There is life to the place, a certain humid vitality. Someone is singing in a bar. Old men are playing dominoes on a patio. Flickering TV and radio babel from terraced apartment buildings.

Coriolanus, bearded now, moves through the streets.

He takes in the life of the town as he walks. Studying the faces of the Volscians around him.

Coriolanus sees a heavily-guarded apartment building at the end of the street. Jeeps and SOLDIERS.

Coriolanus approaches with stealth, moving in and out of shadows along the street, ducking into doorways and alleys, taking advantage of the darkness.

He stops. Steps into the shadows. For he sees...

Aufidius.

Walking with a few of his officers.

Aufidius is beloved in Antium. He has an easy manner with the people. He stops and chats. Laughs with them. He dances for a moment with a little girl.

Coriolanus watches from the shadows, his expression complex. There is real envy ... Aufidius has such a comfortable way with the common people, he's natural, unaffected.

Aufidius jokes with the little girl's parents for a moment and then moves on.

Coriolanus watches Aufidius and his men go into an apartment building.

He scans the building with the eye of a Special Forces soldier. He sees that the soldiers guarding the building are bored, it is perfunctory work.

52   INT. APARTMENT BUILDING-CORRIDOR - NIGHT   52

Coriolanus moves again with stealth, heading toward what is clearly the center of the action: a noisy room on the second floor.

The doorway is guarded by two serious GUARDS. These are not the bored soldiers out front, these are grim and intense warriors.

Coriolanus considers his course.

Decides. Takes a breath. Focuses.

He is like ice now.

He moves--

A steady stride--

He walks right up to the Guards--

Before they can even respond--

He punches one HARD in the throat -- the Guard recoils, gasping for air--

Simultaneously, Coriolanus SLAMS his other hand violently over the entire face of the second Guard -- grabbing his face firmly and SHOVING him back into the door--

So hard that the door slams aside--

And Coriolanus shoves the Guard into--

53   INT. AUFIDIUS' CHAMBER - NIGHT   53

Aufidius is having dinner with some of his men, their wives and some children--

The soldiers bolt up, upsetting the table, smashing dishes -- pulling guns -- alarmed--

As Coriolanus powers in, still holding the second Guard by the face--

He flings the Guard aside--

Aufidius and his men, all pointing weapons at Coriolanus, are stunned.

A long beat.

                    AUFIDIUS
          Whence comes thou? What wouldst thou? Thy
          name?

Coriolanus does not respond.

Aufidius is growing uneasy. His men are tense, ready to open fire at any second.

                    AUFIDIUS
          Speak, man! What's thy name?

                    CORIOLANUS
          A name unmusical to the Volscians' ears,
          And harsh in sound to thine.

The other Guard from outside, and several other soldiers, rush in. Weapons drawn, surrounding Coriolanus.

He doesn't move a muscle.

Aufidius, intrigued by the stranger's courage, waves his men off.

                    AUFIDIUS
          Say, what's thy name?
          Thou has a grim appearance ...What's thy
          name?

                    CORIOLANUS
          Know'st thou me yet?

                    AUFIDIUS
          I know thee not ... Thy name?

                    CORIOLANUS
          My name is Caius Martius, who hath done
          To thee particularly and to all the
          Volsces
          Great hurt and mischief; thereto witness
          may
          My surname ... Coriolanus.

The Volscians look to Aufidius, very nervous, unsure how to proceed. Aufidius just stares back at Coriolanus, staggered.

                    CORIOLANUS
          Only that name remains.

Aufidius doesn't understand. Coriolanus explains:

> CORIOLANUS
> The cruelty and envy of the people,
> Who have all forsook me, hath devoured
> the rest,
> And suffered me by the voice of <u>slaves</u> to
> be
> Whooped out of Rome. Now this extremity
> Hath brought me to thy hearth, not out of
> hope -
> Mistake me not - to save my life; for if
> I had feared death, of all the men in the
> world
> I would have avoided thee, but in mere
> <u>spite</u>,
> To be full quit of those my banishers,
> Stand I before thee here.

Coriolanus dares to take a step toward Aufidius--

The Volscians react. Guns are raised, fingers tight on triggers, an instant from opening fire--

Coriolanus carefully holds out his arms. He's unarmed.

Aufidius nods to his men. They hold their fire.

Coriolanus slowly crosses the room toward Aufidius. Step by step. Their eyes are locked. Nothing else in the world exists.

> CORIOLANUS
> I will fight
> Against my cankered country with the
> spleen
> Of all the under fiends. But if thou
> Dares not this, then I present
> My throat to thee and to thy ancient
> malice...

Coriolanus stops right in front of Aufidius and slowly, carefully, exposes his naked throat.

Bending back his head.

Ready for execution.

> CORIOLANUS
> ... Which not to cut would show thee but
> a fool,
> Since I have ever followed thee with
> hate,
> (MORE)

CORIOLANUS (cont'd)
And cannot live but to thy shame unless
It be to do thee service.

A long beat.

Aufidius stares at Coriolanus.

The Volscians watch, eyes wide, too tense to do anything now.

Aufidius just continues to stare at Coriolanus.

Like lightning -- a blaze of movement--

Aufidius slashes out his distinctive etched knife--

Presses the blade to Coriolanus' naked throat.

The blade presses the skin. A trickle of blood.

Eyes locked.

Coriolanus blinks some sweat from his eyes. This tiny, human
response sparks something in Aufidius.

                    AUFIDIUS
          O Martius ... Martius ...
          Each word thou hast spoke hath weeded
          from my heart
          A root of ancient envy.

He removes his knife from Coriolanus' throat and wipes away
the trace of blood with a finger.

                    AUFIDIUS
          Let me twine
          Mine arms about that body.

He embraces Coriolanus.

Aufidius' men finally relax. Weapons are lowered. Relieved
glances exchanged.

Some of the Volscians, though, are clearly suspicious of
Coriolanus. They watch Aufidius and Coriolanus, concerned.

Aufidius still can't quite believe his ancient enemy is now
his newest ally.

                    AUFIDIUS
          Know thou
          I loved the maid I married; never man
          Sighed truer breath. But that I see thee
          here,
          Thou noble thing, more dances my rapt
                    (MORE)

                         AUFIDIUS (cont'd)
          heart
          Than when I first my wedded mistress saw
          Bestride my threshold.

Coriolanus glances to him, perhaps a little disturbed or
embarrassed by the intensity of Aufidius' words.

Aufidius steps away from him, gestures for Coriolanus to sit.

                         AUFIDIUS
          Why, thou Mars, I tell thee,
          We have a power on foot, and I had
          purpose
          Once more to hew thy target from thy
          brawn,
          Or lose mine arm for it. Thou hast beat
          me out
          Twelve several times, and I have nightly
          since
          Dreamt of encounters 'twixt thyself and
          me.

Aufidius continues quietly, almost whispering:

                         AUFIDIUS
          Worthy Martius,
          Had we no quarrel else to Rome, but that
          Thou art thence banished, we would muster
          all
          From twelve to seventy, and, pouring war
          Into the bowels of ungrateful Rome,
          Like a bold flood, overbear it.

54   INT. SHOWER ROOM - NIGHT   54

Coriolanus sits, naked. He has finally washed off the layers
of dirt from his journey.

An old woman is using an electric razor to shave his head.

Aufidius is standing in the doorway to the room. Watching.
His eyes move over Coriolanus' body, adding up the scars and
wounds.

A pause.

Then Aufidius goes to the old woman. Takes the razor from
her. She goes.

Aufidius continues to shave Coriolanus' head himself.

It is a deeply personal act, even intimate ... Yet Aufidius
employs the same methodical rhythms as when he was sharpening
his knife at the opening of the story.

55   INT. APARTMENT BUILDING-WAR ROOM - NIGHT   55

The Volscian military command center. Maps, recon photos and
radio equipment. Stacks of grenade launchers and arms.

Aufidius' CAPTAINS and AIDES wait alongside some bedraggled
Volsce POLITICIANS in ill-fitting suits.

Aufidius ushers Coriolanus in:

                    AUFIDIUS
          O, come, go in,
          And take our friendly senators by the
          hands.

Coriolanus shakes hands with the politicians:

                    CORIOLANUS
          You bless me, gods.

Then Aufidius takes him to a huge military map laid out on a
pool table. Rome and her territories. Strategic markers
denote Roman forces and Volscian forces.

                    AUFIDIUS
          Therefore, most absolute sir, if thou
          wilt have
          The leading of thine own revenges, take
          The one half of my commission.

The Volscian soldiers and politicos are shocked. Aufidius is
giving Coriolanus command of half his forces!

                    AUFIDIUS
          And set down---
          As best thou art experienced, since thou
          knows
          Thy country's strength and weakness---
          thine own ways,
          Whether to knock against the gates of
          Rome,
          Or rudely visit them in parts remote,
          To fright them ... ere destroy.

Aufidius looks at Coriolanus hard. There it is. The gauntlet
is thrown down. Coriolanus will have to completely betray
Rome: expose her military weaknesses, tell her secrets.

For all his neurotic intensity, Aufidius is a shrewd man.

Coriolanus nods and turns to the battle map, moving various markers around to show Rome's defensive positions.

Aufidius watches him with Machiavellian calm.

56   INT. POLITICO BAR - DAY   56

Several weeks later, back in Rome, politics go on as usual.

Menenius is passing the Tribunes' table. They josh with him:

                    BRUTUS
          Is this Menenius?

                    SICINIUS
          'Tis he,'tis he! O, he is grown most kind
          of late. Hail sir!

                    MENENIUS
          Hail to you both.

                    SICINIUS
          Your Coriolanus
          Is not much missed, but with his friends.

                    MENENIUS
          All's well, and might have been much
          better if
          He could have temporized.

                    SICINIUS
          Where is he, hear you?

                    MENENIUS
          Nay, I hear nothing. His mother and his
          wife
          Hear nothing from him.

                    BRUTUS
          Caius Martius was
          A worthy officer in the war, but
          insolent,
          Overcome with pride, ambitious past all
          thinking,
          Self-loving--

                    MENENIUS
          I think not so.

                    SICINIUS
        And Rome sits safe and still without him.

They are distracted when people begin talking loudly,
alarmed, at the bar. They hush each other and watch the TV
over the bar. Something has happened.

On the TV: a SPECIAL REPORT. Breaking News. A scroll across
the bottom of the screen reads "The Volscians On The March?"

                    TV ANCHORMAN
                 (on TV)
        ... Reports the Volsces with two several
        powers
        Are entered in the Roman territories,
        And with the deepest malice of the war
        Destroy what lies before them...

The whole bar is growing quiet now. All watching the TV,
which shows grainy indistinct images -- like cell phone
pictures -- of troops and tanks.

                    MENENIUS
        'Tis Aufidius,
        Who, hearing of our Martius' banishment,
        Thrusts forth his horns again into the
        world.

                    SICINIUS
                 (nervous)
        Come, what talk you of Martius?

                    BRUTUS
        It cannot be the Volsces dare break with
        us.

                    TV ANCHORMAN
                 (on TV)
        The nobles in great earnestness are going
        All to the Senate House. Some news is
        coming
        That turns their countenances...
                 (he listens to his ear
                  piece for a second)
        Yes, the first report is seconded, and
        more,
        More fearful, is delivered.

The TV picture switches to a flustered TV REPORTER outside
the Senate. A lot of nervous activity behind him.

> TV REPORTER
> (on TV)
> It is spoke freely out of many mouths -
> How probable I do not know - that <u>Martius</u>
> Has <u>joined</u> with Aufidius--

There is an audible gasp in the bar -- quickly silenced and hushed so all can hear the TV:

> TV REPORTER
> (on TV)
> --He leads a power against Rome,
> And vows revenge as spacious as between
> The youngest and oldest thing.

Something close to terror on the faces of the politicos. Menenius, without a word, goes.

He does not want to believe this is possible.

57   INT. VILLA -- BEDROOM - NIGHT   57

Virgilia lies on her bed.

On the TV an imbedded WAR CORRESPONDENT is giving an update, intercut with shaky and unclear images of the Volscian army on the move:

> TV WAR CORRESPONDENT
> (on TV)
> A fearful army, led by Caius Martius
> Associated with Aufidius, rages
> Upon our territories, and have already
> Overborne their way, consumed with fire,
> and took
> What lay before them.

58   INT. VILLA -- LIVING ROOM - NIGHT   58

Volumnia sits, almost frozen, watching the TV. Her emotions are deep and dark.

Her son, to her the model of all Roman virtues, has betrayed his country.

> TV WAR CORRESPONDENT
> (on TV)
> Martius has joined with the Volscians -
> He is their god. He leads them like
> Boys pursuing summer butterflies
> Or butchers killing flies.

Close up on Volumnia's face.

She gives away practically nothing.

59   EXT. VOLSCIAN CAMP - NIGHT   59

Urban industrial wasteland. Old factories and abandoned
warehouses. Broken asphalt. Smashed windows.

The Volscians have set up camp here. On the decaying fringes
of the city. We see military hardware. Guns. Missile
launchers. Armored vehicles.

Soldiers are cleaning weapons, cooking meals, sleeping,
playing video games.

Then...

An incongruous sight...

An old barber chair floats past. Moving across the night sky.
Carried overhead by a group of Volscian soldiers.

But there is something _different_ about these Volscian
soldiers. They have altered their uniforms into something
pagan and primitive. All have shaved heads. Many have face
tattoos or wear striking war paint.

It is like something from LORD OF THE FLIES.

They set the barber chair down outside an abandoned factory.
This shattered and abandoned factory is Coriolanus' domain.
It is decorated with human skulls.

The CAMP BARBER, a fat man in a greasy butcher's apron,
begins to strop his razor.

Hard core young soldiers line up to have their heads shaved.
They are Coriolanus' ACOLYTES.

There is no sign of Coriolanus himself.

Aufidius and his LIEUTENANT stand on the fringes, disturbed
by the strange cult of personality that has grown up around
Coriolanus.

                    AUFIDIUS
          Do they still fly to Coriolanus?

                    LIEUTENANT
          I do not know what witchcraft's in him,
          but
                    (MORE)

> LIEUTENANT (cont'd)
> Your soldiers use him as the grace before
> meat,
> Their talk at table, and their thanks at
> end.
> And you are darkened in this action, sir.

> AUFIDIUS
> He bears himself more proud,
> Even to my person, than I thought he
> would
> When first I did embrace him.

They turn and walk to the building where Aufidius is
quartered:

> LIEUTENANT
> Sir, I beseech you, think you he'll carry
> Rome?

> AUFIDIUS
> (grim)
> I think he'll be to Rome
> As is the osprey to the fish, who takes
> it
> By sovereignty of nature.

Aufidius nods to the guards outside his quarters and enters
with his Lieutenant...

60   INT. VOLSCIAN CAMP-AUFIDIUS' QUARTERS - NIGHT   60

A shattered building. Old graffiti on the walls. Weapons.
Maps. Aufidius' gear.

Aufidius sits on his cot, deep in thought.

He pulls a folded bit of paper from his pocket. Carefully and
lovingly unfolds it. He has been carrying this paper for
months.

It is a glossy magazine cover with a picture of Coriolanus.

He gazes at the picture, his fingers smoothing the paper,
tracing the contours of Coriolanus' face...

> AUFIDIUS
> Whether t'was pride,
> Whether defect of judgement,
> Or whether nature,
> Not to be other than one thing,
> Made him feared,
> So hated, and so banished.

A beat as he studies the picture.

His lieutenant watches him closely, disturbed by Aufidius'
obsession with Coriolanus.

>   AUFIDIUS
>   So our virtues
>   Lie in the interpretation of the time.

He brings the picture closer, whispering now:

>   AUFIDIUS
>   One fire drives out one fire; one nail,
>   one nail;
>   Rights by rights founder, strengths by
>   strengths do fail ...
>   And when, Caius, Rome is thine,
>   Thou art poorest of all -- then shortly
>   art thou mine.

61   INT. ROMAN WAR ROOM - NIGHT   61

Rome is at war now, so the room is busy and tense. Maps and
video footage chart the enemy's progress. Soldiers confer
urgently outside the door.

Menenius stands with the two Tribunes, Brutus and Sicinius.
With them are several SENATORS and GENERALS.

Menenius snaps angrily:

>   MENENIUS
>   No, I'll not go!

>   SICINIUS
>   (imploring)
>   Good Menenius--

>   MENENIUS
>   Go, you that banished him!
>   A mile before his tent fall down, and
>   knee
>   The way into his mercy.

They stop when Titus enters with General Cominius.

Titus is dusty, has just come from somewhere. He is pale.
Truly shaken.

Menenius and the others crowd around him, waiting for his
report.

STILLS

Ralph Fiennes stars as Caius Martius "Coriolanus"

Photographs by Larry D. Horricks

Ralph Fiennes (Caius Martius "Coriolanus")

Gerard Butler (Tullus Aufidius)

Vanessa Redgrave (Volumnia)

Jessica Chastain (Virgilia)

Brian Cox (Menenius)

John Kani (General Cominius)

Gerard Butler (Tullus Aufidius)

Ralph Fiennes (Caius Martius "Coriolanus")

Left to right: John Kani (General Cominius), Vanessa Redgrave (Volumnia),
Ralph Fiennes (Caius Martius Coriolanus), Jessica Chastain (Virgilia), and
Harry Fenn (Young Martius)

Ralph Fiennes (Caius Martius "Coriolanus") and Vanessa Redgrave
(Volumnia)

Lubna Azabal (Tamora)

Lubna Azabal (Tamora) and James Nesbitt (Sicinius)

Gerard Butler (Tullus Aufidius) and Ralph Fiennes (Caius Martius "Coriolanus")

Ralph Fiennes (Caius Martius "Coriolanus") and Gerard Butler (Tullus Aufidius)

Ralph Fiennes (Caius Martius "Coriolanus") and Jessica Chastain (Virgilia)

Ralph Fiennes (Caius Martius "Coriolanus"), Gerard Butler (Tullus Aufidius) and Vanessa Redgrave (Volumnia)

Ralph Fiennes (Caius Martius "Coriolanus")

Gerard Butler (Tullus Aufidius)

Ralph Fiennes directing

Titus sits, takes a moment to pull himself together, and then reports with the grim severity of a death sentence:

> TITUS
> He would not seem to know me.

A beat.

> TITUS
> I urged our old acquaintance, and the drops
> That we have bled together. "Coriolanus"
> He would not answer to, forbade all names...

A long beat. They wait for him to go on.

Titus searches for the words to continue.

> TITUS
> He was ... a kind of nothing.
> (a difficult beat)
> Titleless...
> Till he had forged himself a name in the fire
> Of burning Rome.

He has no more to say, his head drops.

Menenius begins to leave the room. The Tribunes stop him, leading him to a secluded corner:

> SICINIUS
> If you refuse your aid
> In this--

> BRUTUS
> If you
> Would be your country's pleader, your good tongue,
> More than the instant army we can make,
> Might stop our countryman.

> MENENIUS
> No, I'll not meddle.

> SICINIUS
> Pray you, go to him.

> MENENIUS
> What should I do?

Brutus stops him, with real emotion:

> BRUTUS
> Only make trial what your love can do
> For Rome towards Martius.

> MENENIUS
> Well, and say that Martius
> Return me, as Titus is returned,
> Unheard - what then?

> SICINIUS
> Yet your good will
> Must have that thanks from Rome.

Menenius thinks about it.

> COMINIUS
> You know the very road into his kindness,
> And cannot lose your way.

Menenius, despite all still a patriot at heart, decides.

> MENENIUS
> I'll undertake it ...
> I think he'll hear me.

The Tribunes are relieved. Cominius nods and escorts Menenius out.

Brutus and Sicinius return to Titus.

> TITUS
> He'll never hear him.

> SICINIUS
> No?

> TITUS
> I tell you, he does sit in gold, his eye
> Red as it would burn Rome.

62   EXT. CHECKPOINT-HIGHWAY - NIGHT   62

The Roman checkpoint on the desolate highway. A formidable military presence here now: soldiers, heavy weapons, tanks.

Volscian troops and a jeep can be seen down the highway.

We see Menenius' limousine pull up.

He and General Cominius climb out. Menenius is out of place in his trim business suit: a politician among soldiers.

Menenius steels himself then passes through the Roman
checkpoint.

He walks down the highway toward the distant Volscian troops.

63   EXT. VOLSCIAN CAMP - NIGHT   63

Menenius is blindfolded, roughly pulled by two Volscian
soldiers.

We hear some of the soldiers hooting at him. We stay close on
Menenius' blindfolded face, sharing his feeling of
disorientation and suspense.

The Volscians drag him into the abandoned factory--

64   INT. ABANDONED FACTORY - NIGHT   64

Finally his guards stop him and pull off his blindfold--

Revealing--

Coriolanus. Transformed.

And terrifying.

He is no longer Roman. He is not Volscian. He is, as Titus
said, "a kind of nothing."

He sits in the barber chair. His head is completely shaved.
His face is marked with martial face painting. These striking
totemic markings also cover his scarred body.

He is primitive. Inhuman. Like a dragon.

The Angel of Death.

His young warrior Acolytes -- similarly shaved and painted --
are gathered around him; his personal bodyguard and cult.

A long beat as Menenius stares at his friend, stunned at the
pagan metamorphosis.

Coriolanus just gazes back at him.

Menenius finally pulls himself together and approaches, with
fulsome bravado:

                    MENENIUS
          The glorious gods sit in hourly synod
          about thy particular prosperity, and love
                    (MORE)

                    MENENIUS (cont'd)
          thee no worse than thy old friend
          Menenius does! O Martius, Martius!

He steps forward to hug Coriolanus. Two of the Acolytes stop
him. He can approach no further.

Menenius accepts this. No matter. He is completely confident
he will be able to manipulate his protege. He always has in
the past.

                    MENENIUS
          Thou art preparing fire for us. Look
          thee, here's water to quench it. I was
          hardly moved to come to thee, but being
          assured none but myself could move
          thee, I have been blown out of your gates
          with sighs, and conjure thee to pardon
          Rome.

A long beat.

Menenius waits for an answer. Grows uneasy.

Then...

                    CORIOLANUS
          Away.

                    MENENIUS
          How? ... Away?

                    CORIOLANUS
              (ice)
          Wife ... mother ... child ... I know not.
          My affairs
          Are servanted to others.

Menenius can't believe this cold response--

                    MENENIUS
          Sir--

                    CORIOLANUS
          Therefore be gone.

His frigid eyes slice into Menenius:

                    CORIOLANUS
          Another word, Menenius,
          I will not hear thee speak.

Menenius stares at him, shaken to the core.

The Guards pull Menenius away.

Coriolanus doesn't even glance at him.

65   EXT. CHECKPOINT-HIGHWAY - DAWN   65

The sun is just rising. Back at the Roman checkpoint,
Menenius strides toward his limousine. He has been deeply
shaken by his interaction with the transformed Coriolanus.

General Cominius follows urgently, Menenius doesn't stop:

                    MENENIUS
          This Martius is grown from man to dragon.
          He has wings; he's more than a creeping
          thing.

He stops at his limo.

A beat.

He turns back to Cominius. We see the pain in Menenius' eyes.

                    MENENIUS
          There is no more mercy in him than there
          is milk in a male tiger.

He climbs into his limo. Shuts the door.

The limousine drives off, sending up a cloud of dust that
swirls around Cominius.

66   INT. MENENIUS' LIMO - DAWN   66

Menenius sits in the back of his limo as it speeds back to
Rome.

The rejection by Coriolanus has wounded him. Also he is
plagued by guilt. He helped create this monster. He pushed
Coriolanus into politics. And now Coriolanus has lost his
soul, even his humanity, and Rome is to be put to the sword.
All his fault.

This preys on him.

67   EXT. TRAIN TRACKS - MORNING   67

Menenius' limousine pulls over by an isolated set of railroad
tracks. Weeds springing up. Battered advertising posters. An
old chain link fence.

Menenius climbs out of the car and walks along the tracks.
Thinking.

He stops.

He sits on the railroad tracks.

Pulls out a little pocket knife and, in the Roman fashion,
efficiently slits his wrists.

He stares out over the hideous landscape.

Blood begins to pool around his stylish shoes.

From afar we see him, sitting on the railroad tracks, alone
and forlorn in this surreal urban wasteland, like a Samuel
Beckett character.

He slumps over.

Menenius is dead.

68   EXT. VOLSCIAN CAMP - DAY   68

Volumnia, Virgilia and Young Martius stride past the soldiers
and mountains of military hardware. Volumnia leads, pulling
the others by the hand.

Some of the soldiers whistle. Some spit. Others laugh and
make lascivious noises. Many just watch with grim dislike.

Volumnia appears to be completely impervious to the whistles
and cruel taunts. Her head is high, back straight, eagle eye
forward. She was never more a Roman patrician.

She is magnificent.

69   INT. ABANDONED FACTORY - DAY   69

Coriolanus stands as Volumnia, Virgilia and Young Martius are
led into the factory.

He tries to register nothing, assuming a sort of glacial
calm.

Volumnia and the others stop -- taking in Coriolanus' savage
new demeanor and appearance -- taking in the Acolytes and
pagan totems.

Volumnia just stands, peering sternly at her son. As if
daring him not to crumble before her. He doesn't.

Aufidius watches everything closely.

It is Virgilia, finally, who bravely approaches:

                    VIRGILIA
          My lord and husband--

He stops her, almost a warning, with:

                    CORIOLANUS
          These eyes are not the same I wore in
          Rome.

                    VIRGILIA
          The sorrow that delivers us thus changed
          Makes you think so.

                    CORIOLANUS
          Best of my flesh,
          Forgive my tyranny, but do not say
          For that "Forgive our Romans."

She shows great courage. Stepping forward and kissing him
deeply. A long kiss.

                    CORIOLANUS
          O, a kiss ... Long as my exile, sweet as
          my revenge.

It is a perverse response. In his monomaniacal imagination,
his wife's kiss is obsessively equated with his revenge on
Rome.

He finally moves to Volumnia, simply can't resist her orbital
pull.

                    CORIOLANUS
          You gods ... I prate,
          And the most noble mother of the world
          Leave unsaluted. Sink, my knee, in the
          earth.

He kneels before her. It is done with a sense of duty and
protocol, not affection.

                    VOLUMNIA
          O, stand up blest.

He rises.

                    VOLUMNIA
          Then with no softer cushion than the
          flint
          I kneel before thee.

She quickly and dramatically kneels before him. It is a coup
de theatre and a masterpiece of manipulation.

                    CORIOLANUS
          What is this?
          Your knees to me? To your corrected son?

                    VOLUMNIA
          Thou art my warrior;
          I hope to frame thee.

She indicates Young Martius:

                    VOLUMNIA
          This is a poor epitome of yours,
          Which by the interpretation of full time
          May show like all yourself.

                    CORIOLANUS
               (to his son)
          The god of soldiers,
          Inform thy thoughts with nobleness, that
          thou may prove
          To shame invulnerable.

Volumnia pulls Young Martius down:

                    VOLUMNIA
          Your knee, sir.

She pulls Virgilia down:

                    VOLUMNIA
          Even he, your wife, and myself,
          Are suitors to you.

All three kneel before Coriolanus. A pitiable sight. But he
has no pity.

He turns, sits in the barber chair.

                    CORIOLANUS
          I beseech you, peace!
          Or, if you'd ask, remember this:
          Do not bid me dismiss my soldiers, or
          capitulate
          Again with Rome's mechanics. Tell me not
          Wherein I seem unnatural. Desire not
                    (MORE)

                    CORIOLANUS (cont'd)
          To ally my rages and revenges with
          Your colder reasons.

Volumnia stands, assuming again a position of strength.

                    VOLUMNIA
          O, no more, no more!
          You have said you will not grant us
          anything,
          For we have nothing else to ask but that
          Which you deny already; yet we will ask,
          That, if you fail in our request, the
          blame
          May hang upon your hardness. <u>Therefore</u>
          <u>hear</u> <u>us</u>.

                    CORIOLANUS
          Aufidius, and you Volsces, mark; for
          we'll
          Hear naught from Rome in private.
                    (coldly, to her)
          Your request?

                    VOLUMNIA
          Should we be silent and not speak, our
          raiment
          And state of bodies would reveal what
          life
          We have led since thy exile. Think with
          thyself
          How more unfortunate than all living
          women
          Are we come hither, since that thy sight,
          which should
          Make our eyes flow with joy, hearts dance
          with comforts,
          Constrains them weep and shake with fear
          and sorrow,
          Making the mother, wife, and child to see
          The son, the husband and the father
          tearing
          His country's bowels out.

Coriolanus' face is a study in aloof neutrality. Yet he is
listening intensely and Volumnia's words are affecting.

She fights back emotion. It is impossible to tell if this
real or feigned.

                    VOLUMNIA
          For myself, son,
          I propose not to wait on fortune till
          These wars determine. If I cannot
          persuade thee
                    (MORE)

                    VOLUMNIA (cont'd)
          Rather to show a noble grace, thou shalt
          no sooner
          March to assault thy country than to
          Tread on thy mother's womb
          That brought thee to this world.

                    VIRGILIA
                    (stands)
          Ay, and mine,
          That brought you forth this boy, to keep
          your name
          Living to time.

Young Martius stands as well and approaches his father,
challenging and warlike:

                    YOUNG MARTIUS
          You shall not tread on me.
          I'll run away till I am bigger, but then
          I'll fight!

Coriolanus stares at him -- the intensity of the boy's
aggression is disturbing. And familiar.

                    CORIOLANUS
          I have sat too long.

He rises and turns as if to go--

                    VOLUMNIA
          Nay, go not from us thus!

Her command stops him. She appeals, quickly getting to the
point of her argument:

                    VOLUMNIA
          If it were so that our request did tend
          To save the Romans, thereby to destroy
          The Volsces whom you serve, you might
          condemn us
          As poisonous of your honor. No, our suit
          Is that you reconcile them -- so the
          Volsces
          May say "This mercy we have showed," the
          Romans,
          "This we received," and each in either
          side
          Give the all-hail to thee and cry, "Be
          blest
          For making up this peace!"

Coriolanus does not respond.

She softens...

                      VOLUMNIA
          Speak to me, son...

Still he does not respond.

His emotions are roiling.

Still she is soft and vulnerable...

                      VOLUMNIA
          Why dost not speak?

But softness is not a note she plays naturally. She knows it.

Her natural aggressiveness comes out, anger and outrage
gradually boiling to the surface:

                      VOLUMNIA
          Thinks thou it honorable for a noble man
          Still to remember wrongs? Daughter, speak
          you.
          He cares not for your weeping. Speak
          thou, boy.
          Perhaps thy childishness will move him
          more
          Than can our reasons. There's no man in
          the world
          More bound to his mother, yet here he
          lets me prate
          Like one in the stocks!

She is assaulting him now, on the attack:

                      VOLUMNIA
          Thou hast never in thy life
          Showed thy dear mother any courtesy,
          When she, poor hen,
          Has clucked thee to the wars and safely
          home
          Loaded with honor. Say my request's
          unjust,
          And spurn me back; and the gods will
          plague thee,
          That thou restrains from me the duty
          which
          To a mother's part belongs!

Coriolanus can take no more, turns and begins to walk away--

Volumnia reacts like lightning -- grabbing Virgilia and Young
Martius and dragging them to the dirt with her--

                    VOLUMNIA
          Down! Let us shame him with our knees!

She claws at the dirt -- like Hecuba -- keening -- a shocking
explosion of raw emotion -- almost an incantation:

                    VOLUMNIA
          Down! An end! This is the last. So we
          will home to Rome,
          And die among our neighbors. Nay, behold!
          This boy, that cannot tell what he would
          have
          But kneels and holds up hands for
          fellowship,
          Does reason our petition with more
          strength
          Than thou hast to deny it.

She remains kneeling, panting for air.

Coriolanus looks at her. His noble mother. Clawing in the
dirt like an animal. Filthy. Despairing. Her face wet with
tears.

She looks back up at him. She senses she has failed.

It's over.

                    VOLUMNIA
          Come, let us go.

She rises slowly, her age showing. Her spirit broken. Or
seeming so.

She summons up all her strength for a lacerating and icy
farewell:

                    VOLUMNIA
          This fellow had a Volscian to his mother;
          His wife is in Corioles and his child
          Like him by chance ... Yet give us our
          dispatch.
          I am hushed until our city be afire,
          And then I'll speak a little.

She turns and begins to go.

But...

We finally see Coriolanus crack.

Like a great building crumbling.

Like fissures cutting across marble.

Emotion floods into him.

He lunges forward and grabs her hand. Volumnia stops.

>   CORIOLANUS
>   O mother ... mother...
>   What have you done?

He falls to his knees, clutching her hand.

>   CORIOLANUS
>   Behold, the heavens do ope,
>   The gods look down -- and this unnatural
>   scene
>   They laugh at.

He buries his head in her, like a lost child:

>   CORIOLANUS
>   O my mother, mother! O!
>   You have won a happy victory for Rome;
>   But for your son - believe it, O believe
>   it! -
>   Most dangerously you have with him
>   prevailed ...
>   (he looks up at her
>   deeply)
>   If not most mortal to him.

She looks down at him. His meaning, his foreshadowing, is
clear: she has saved Rome, but he knows he is doomed. Rome
will live. He will die. This is the price for her victory
today.

She is willing to pay that price. So is he.

A moment between them.

He accepts his destiny.

>   CORIOLANUS
>   But let it come.

He stands, regains his composure. He slowly walks to
Aufidius.

He leans close, speaking intimately:

>   CORIOLANUS
>   Aufidius, though I cannot make true wars,
>   I'll frame convenient peace. Now, good
>   (MORE)

                         CORIOLANUS (cont'd)
          Aufidius,
          Were you in my stead, would you have
          heard
          A mother less? Or granted less? ...
          Aufidius?

                         AUFIDIUS
                    (carefully)
          I was moved withal.

                         CORIOLANUS
          I dare be sworn you were.
          And, sir, it is no little thing to make
          Mine eyes to sweat compassion. But, good
          sir,
          What peace you'll make, advise me.

We study Aufidius' face. He gives away nothing.

Coriolanus turns back to Volumnia. Looks at her.

She is victorious.

And we go to...

70   INT. FORMAL MINISTRY HALL - DAY   70

A solemn peace treaty signing ceremony.

Coriolanus represents the Volscians. Cominius represents the
Romans. They sit side-by-side at desks signing the treaty.

Volumnia and Virgilia, gorgeously dressed, are present. So
too Brutus and Sicinius. The press films everything.

It has the stiff formality of a White House ceremony.

Cominius concludes signing:

                         COMINIUS
          A merrier day did never yet greet Rome,
          No, not the expulsion of the Tarquins.
          We have all
          Great cause to give great thanks.

He looks to Volumnia.

                         COMINIUS
          Behold our patroness, the life of Rome.

She is erect and exalted. "The Life of Rome" personified.

She ignores her son.

Coriolanus will not look at her.

71   EXT. TRUCK STOP - DAY   71

A rundown Truck Stop in an industrial wasteland.

Garish, buzzing neon. Filthy 18-wheelers refueling. Music
droning from a radio.

Aufidius, his Lieutenant and seven of his men are waiting
outside the dusty diner.

The men with Aufidius are thugs and killers, the most brutal
Volsces he could find. We note a couple of Coriolanus'
Acolytes among them. They have turned with great venom on
their hero.

They are like a mafia hit squad, waiting for Coriolanus to
return with the peace treaty.

Aufidius is deep in thought.

His Lieutenant breaks the silence:

                    LIEUTENANT
          How is it with our general?

                    AUFIDIUS
          As with a man by his own charity slain.

                    LIEUTENANT
          Our soldiers will remain uncertain whilst
          'Twixt you there's difference; but the
          fall of either
          Makes the survivor heir of <u>all</u>.

                    AUFIDIUS
          I know it,
          And my pretext to strike at him admits
          A good construction.

A beat. He continues more to himself than them, almost
convincing himself.

                    AUFIDIUS
          I raised him, and I pawned
          Mine honor for his truth; who being so
          heightened,
          He watered his new plants with dews of
          flattery,
          Seducing so my friends.
                    (bitterly)
                    (MORE)

                    AUFIDIUS (cont'd)
At the last
I seemed his <u>follower</u>, not partner, and
He waged me with his countenance as if
I had been <u>mercenary</u>.

                    LIEUTENANT
So he did, my lord.
The army marveled at it; and in the last,
When he had carried Rome and that we
looked
For no less spoil than glory--

Aufidius works himself into a neurotic intensity:

                    AUFIDIUS
There was it!
For which my sinews shall be stretched
upon him.
At a few drops of <u>women's</u> <u>rheum</u>, which
are
As cheap as lies, he sold the blood and
labor
Of our great action -- <u>Therefore</u> <u>shall</u> <u>he</u>
<u>die</u>,
And I'll renew me in his fall.

                    LIEUTENANT
Therefore, at your vantage,
Ere he express himself or move the people
With what he would say, let him feel your
sword,
Which we will second.

                    AUFIDIUS
              (sees something)
Say no more.

In the distance they can see a Roman military truck
approaching. Clouds of dust billow up.

They exchange a look. This is what they have been waiting
for. They stand, stretch and prepare.

The truck stops across the highway from them and Coriolanus
gets out. He is unarmed.

He stops.

He sees Aufidius and the thugs. Waiting for him. Like a death
squad.

Coriolanus looks at them.

He knows exactly what's going to happen.

He is ready.

He nods and the truck drives off.

Coriolanus slowly crosses the highway to the truck stop, like a gunslinger walking down Main Street.

There is something new to Coriolanus here. A sort of acceptance. He knows his time is past.

Aufidius and the thugs go to meet him. The thugs spread out a bit, strategically, getting ready to strike. Coriolanus' experienced eyes miss none of this.

> CORIOLANUS
> (to Aufidius)
> I am returned your soldier,
> No more infected with my country's love
> Than when I parted hence, but still subsisting
> Under your great command.
> We have made peace
> With no less honor to the Volscians
> Than shame to the Romans.

> AUFIDIUS
> Tell the <u>traitor</u>, in the highest degree
> He hath abused your powers.

Coriolanus is ready for Aufidius' ploy. He is amused at the obvious attempt to anger him:

> CORIOLANUS
> Traitor? How now?

> AUFIDIUS
> Ay, traitor, <u>Martius</u>.

> CORIOLANUS
> "Martius"?

> AUFIDIUS
> Ay, Martius, Caius Martius! Dost thou think
> I'll grace thee with that robbery, thy stolen name
> "Coriolanus"?

He spins to the others, making the case against Coriolanus with cutting bitterness:

                    AUFIDIUS
          Perfidiously
          He has betrayed your business and given
          up,
          For certain drops of salt, your city Rome-
          I say "your city" - to his wife and
          mother;
          Breaking his oath and resolution, like
          A twist of rotten silk; never admitting
          Counsel of the war, but at his nurse's
          tears
          He whined and roared away your victory!

Coriolanus tries to contain his anger:

                    CORIOLANUS
          Hear'st thou, Mars?

                    AUFIDIUS
          Name not the god, thou boy of tears.

                    CORIOLANUS
          Measureless liar, thou has made my heart
          Too great for what contains it. "Boy"? O
          slave.

Coriolanus' eyes miss nothing ... a Volscian thug shifting
... a bead of sweat on another ... one secretly reaching into
his coat for a weapon.

Some of the Volscian thugs are clearly nervous.

Coriolanus is ready. He prepares himself mentally to die. He
is acutely controlled:

                    CORIOLANUS
          Cut me to pieces, Volsces.
          Men and lads, stain all your edges on me.

It is a dare. A challenge.

                    CORIOLANUS
          "Boy"? False hound.
          If you have writ your annals true, 'tis
          there
          That, like an eagle in a dovecote, I
          Fluttered your Volscians in Corioles.

His gaze burns into Aufidius:

                    CORIOLANUS
          Alone I did it ... "Boy."

                            AUFIDIUS
                     Let him die for it.

At this command, his men move--

Aufidius steps back as--

The Volscian thugs attack--

With knives, machetes and tire irons--

Coriolanus fights bravely -- disarming two, grabbing their
weapons, killing them, fighting back--

Slashing and cutting his way through the killers--

Closer and closer to Aufidius, who just watches--

Blood spattering and spraying--

But the thugs overpower Coriolanus, there are just too many--

They stab him -- slicing with knives -- battering with chains
and clubs--

It is graceless and brutal carnage.

Slaughter.

But still he comes on. Body cut to bits. He refuses to fall.
Like something immortal. An obscene demon of blood.

Finally the thugs move away.

Coriolanus still stands. Teetering. His face is a swollen
mask of blood and gore. Blood flows from his body, pooling
around his feet.

Aufidius steps forward.

What is left of Coriolanus glares at him through blood.

Aufidius slowly pulls his knife. The same knife he was
sharpening so carefully at the opening of the story. It has
finally found its purpose.

Coriolanus looks at him.

Aufidius steps to him. Takes his neck. Pulls him onto the
knife. Driving it into him. Cradling his head like a lover.

They stand like this.

Then Aufidius gently lowers his body to the ground.

The lonely whistle of the wind.

Abrupt cut to--

72   EXT. TRUCK - DAY   72

Coriolanus' body is awkwardly tossed into the back of an open truck. Like a sack of potatoes.

Sprawled ungainly in death.

No ritual or ceremony. No honor.

Snap to black.

The End.

SCENE NOTES

BY JOHN LOGAN

SCENE 1 (AUFIDIUS SHARPENS HIS KNIFE)

The opening image and line of a movie are particularly important to me. They are like an overture: an opportunity to set the tone and mood of the piece, to help establish the visual and aural vocabulary for the viewer. No one does openings like Shakespeare. Consider the first line of *Hamlet*, a play about a man questioning his deepest identity: "Who's there?" Or the first word of *Richard III*, about a man who has been waiting impatiently his whole life, like a snake coiling to strike, until this very moment: "*Now* ... is the winter of our discontent."

We played with all manner of openings for this film. For a while I showed Coriolanus riding a white horse, man and beast, man *as* beast, the Imperial animal. ("Nature teaches beasts to know their own." Act II, Scene 1.) Wasn't right: too symbolic and visually cold for the heat of the storytelling. Then I explored images of Coriolanus' son chasing a butterfly and ripping it to pieces, an unforgettable image from the play. Also wasn't right: too remote and intimate for the scope of the piece and too removed from the central characters. Finally the idea of a blade emerged, marked with totemic etchings: primitive but lethal, modern but classical. The thought that this very blade would be used to finally kill Coriolanus after his Rasputin-like fight for life at the end provided a final dramatic resonance that made this the necessary beginning.

As importantly, starting with Coriolanus' nemesis, Aufidius, allowed us to set up that neurotic relationship from the first frames of the movie. We see that Aufidius is intently watching Coriolanus on TV as he works, so the audience knows in some way that this is going to be a story about these two men working out their destiny.

SCENE 8 (ATROCITY VIDEO)

Although the murder of the young Roman prisoner is written as a throat slashing, we changed it to a gunshot right before filming. The idea was that the release of this video would shock complacent Rome, much as the release of images of modern atrocities can incite terror and action in moribund governments. The horrific, loud echo of the gunshot in that tiny cavern room gave an aural punch and exclamation point to the vicious act.

SCENE 12 (THE BATTLE)

When planning out the battle of Corioles, Ralph Fiennes and I looked at countless visual images to suggest the tone we were looking for: gritty and modern urban warfare. Something chaotic at the heart, but with specific human moments that linger. We studied pictures from the Balkans, the Iraq War, Northern Ireland, Somalia, and other modern conflicts. *The Battle for Algiers* is a movie we spoke about when working on this part of the script. (This movie is highly recommended for anyone who wants to write film action with the sting of truth. Also recommended are the recent *Carlos the Jackal* and my friend Kathryn Bigelow's majestic *The Hurt Locker,* which, like *Coriolanus,* was shot by the great cinematographer Barry Ackroyd.) It's absolutely imperative when you're writing an action sequence to be specific, and not give generalized moods or images that don't translate eventually to something visual. Also to make sure you're telling a *story* in the sequence, not just indulging in special effects or visceral action or random stunts—that's pornography, not drama. This is where working closely with a director is vital. You need to tease out the story of the action as it relates to the characters first and foremost, and then find ways to dramatize it. It's not enough to say a character is a brutal killer, you must show him brutally killing. I always think about Fred Astaire when I write action scenes because he was the first movie dancer to insist that his big musical numbers always had to move the story along. Narrative momentum is everything in movies; showmanship comes second.

Shakespeare's battles always surprise me on stage. He is the absolute master of finding the well-observed human detail that makes the battles true and terrible. He never shies away from the human cost of warfare, even in his most seemingly jingoistic plays like *Henry V*. The slaughter of the boys in that play—or Falstaff's wise jokes during the carnage in *Henry IV, Part One*—remind us of the flesh and blood behind all that steel and armor.

In *Coriolanus*, there is a sublime moment after the battle where an exhausted and distracted Coriolanus tells a story of being treated kindly by a poor man in the course of the battle. It's only a few lines, and Shakespeare never dramatizes the moment, but it makes everything on stage feel more real because it is such a small and specific detail. We decided to film that moment. In the midst of our roaring machine gun fire and splattering blood, Coriolanus confronts an old man alone in a seedy little room. The terrified old man gives Coriolanus a bottle of water, which Coriolanus drains, his blood-soaked eyes never leaving the old man. To me, this is the truly Shakespearean moment in our battle scene.

SCENE 19 (CORIOLANUS AND AUFIDIUS FIGHT)
The first confrontation between the hated rivals—Coriolanus and Aufidius—is long, violent and very purposefully homoerotic. One can't read the play without being struck by the charge between these two characters. Ralph and I always talked about the struggle between them here, finally devolving into something like a Francis Bacon painting: two men merged and grappling in something that is partly a hideous death struggle and partly great sex.

SCENE 23 (VOLUMNIA'S VOICE OVER)
To Voice Over or not to Voice Over, that is the question. Invariably in a Shakespearean film adaptation you run into the challenge of the soliloquy. On stage, these direct-address speeches to the audience are riveting drama, and one of the reasons we relish Shakespeare's plays is to have the characters let us into their minds—to be co-conspirators with Iago or Hamlet or Rosalind. We feel particularly close to the characters because they trust us enough to open their hearts and minds; or they feel they can manipulate us to their own ends. But in either case it's a powerfully <u>direct</u> connection. But on screen, there is no live audience. The "us" of the theatre is turned into the impassive viewer of a screen. There is no authentic interaction or connection. So how do you treat the soliloquy on screen?

Various Shakespeare films handle this differently. Sometimes within the same film there are multiple conventions employed. Peter Brook pretty much eliminates the soliloquies from his lyrical and austere version of *King Lear*. Olivier uses Voice Over to present those he retained in his *Hamlet*: the filmic equivalent of the inner monologue. Kenneth Branagh in his version of *Hamlet* (my personal favorite Shakespeare film adaptation) uses both traditional speech to an objective middle-distance as well as Voice Over and other more abstract conventions: Branagh is muscular in using the language of cinema to let Hamlet's soul speak.

The play *Coriolanus* has very few traditional soliloquies. Most of the longer speeches are directly addressed to another character or group of characters. The speech-making, for the most part, is naturalistic. In approaching the film we wanted to avoid traditional Voice Over as the conceit to present inner language or thought. It seemed an old-fashioned device in a movie that was seeking at every turn to give the bite of modernity. It's a polite convention perfectly appropriate to Olivier's stately *Hamlet* but less fitting to our raw and rough Rome. We made two exceptions for language and ideas we thought so important that we just couldn't lose them and thought would actually benefit from being Voice Over. The first is in this scene as the great Volumnia—one of Shakespeare's most unknowable and towering creations—watches her wounded son return from the battle:

> VOLUMNIA (V.O.)
> *Before him*
> *He carries noise, and behind him he leaves tears.*
> *Death, that dark spirit, in his nervy arm doth lie;*
> *Which, being advanced, declines, and then men die.*

We watch Vanessa Redgrave's face as we hear the words. In her eyes we see the awareness and *pride* in her son's power as a death-dealing "dark spirit." The moment would have been weakened if she had spoken the lines to another character—if she had not been alone with her innermost thoughts. In this case, we needed to peer into her soul (her eyes) not as an act of communication with another character, but as a cinematic way to let her thoughts emerge secretly to us. It's too private to be spoken aloud.

SCENE 24 (CORIOLANUS AND VOLUMNIA TOGETHER)

What is Shakespeare's genius in *Coriolanus*? To me it is this: in a play about so many things, and so deeply and murkily about them, the climax is a boy weeping into his mother's arms. It's dead simple. It's not a political or military climax, it's not a grand speech or battle; it's not about the ostensible "issues" of the play. It's a boy and his mom.

The intense and neurotic relationship between Coriolanus and Volumnia is the great private event that runs through the play. The organ note sounds in the very first scene ("... be content to say it was for his country, he did it to please his mother...") and plays through the entire score. When the Freudians finally turned their attention to Shakespeare, this relationship was a particular favorite source of analysis, along with Hamlet and Gertrude. Indeed it would not be too far wrong to say that this play has been more loved by psychologists than audiences over the last hundred years.

So I always knew I would be looking for ways to dramatize the perversely deep and complicated bond between these two characters. How could I show the intimate world they inhabit? How could I show it with the severity and extremity it demanded? First I did what every writer does: I imagined the truth. I let my mind wander as I extrapolated from what Shakespeare tells us to imagine a whole back story. What was their life together? What were the events they shared? What were the moments that shaped their bond? Since Volumnia says she sent him off to the wars when he was a boy, I imagined she would also be the one to bandage his wounds when he came home. Like any mother putting a Band-aid on a kid's cut knee. But in this case it was stab wounds and bullet holes. Her touching his body as she bandaged him was an image that stayed with me because of its obvious intimacy and even inappropriate sensuality. This scene is the result and is my favorite in the film. Vanessa Redgrave and Ralph Fiennes play it to perfection, with just enough awareness of the sensual and the fragile.

Significantly, I wanted the sting at the end of the scene to be the exclusion of Virgilia, Coriolanus' wife, from the private moment. She can never have such a close bond with her husband:

She stops in the doorway. It is embarrassing for her, as if she has interrupted two lovers.
    A long moment.
    She looks to her husband.
    To Volumnia.
    They stare back.
    There is no way she can compete with their intimacy.
    Surrendering, she silently goes.

SCENE 40 ("YOU COMMON CRY OF CURS.")

Coriolanus is not a play crammed with famous Shakespearean speeches. There is no "To be or not to be" or "Tomorrow and tomorrow and tomorrow." The closest we have to a theatrical purple patch is Coriolanus' enraged explosion against the people of Rome after he has been banished:

CORIOLANUS
You common cry of curs!
Whose breath I hate
As reek of the rotten fens, whose loves I prize
As the dead carcasses of unburied men
That do corrupt my air
I banish you…[etc.]

Ralph Fiennes and I spoke a lot about how to approach this particular moment in the story. Many actors try to sidle up to the famous speeches, almost slipping into them casually, so as the audience won't notice they have arrived at "the big speech." I recently saw the wonderful Rory Kinnear play Hamlet at the National Theatre in London. He slipped into "To be or not to be" while casually lighting a cigarette and chatting conversationally. It was magnificent because there was no sense of heightened theatricality around the language and so we weren't pulled out of the play, we were pulled closer, almost seduced into the famous soliloquy as Rory went deeper and deeper into the anguish of it, the depth of the emotion a surprise to both Hamlet and us. I've never seen the speech better.

I felt we needed to take the opposite approach to this moment of the film. One of the (many) dangers in playing Coriolanus is that you end up shouting and angry the whole play—and with little variation it can get oppressive, the audience will stop listening. But this moment is the explosion of all explosions and had to top all the venom expressed previously, and subsequently, by the character. This is also the last moment in the play until the very end that Coriolanus actually gets angry. After this, his fury turns into a more grim determination as he gradually devolves into "a kind of nothing." Ralph and I came to refer to this speech as the moment the dragon finally roars: the great patriot and soldier has been banished; he's been out-foxed by his political opponents and the people of Rome have turned against him. He has lost everything of worth. His next act will be to turn his back on his country, join with his enemy, and attack Rome in vengeance. It has to be a volcanic roar of a speech.

So as a screenwriter, my job was to create a context for Shakespeare's unforgettable speech. I felt opposition was the key: the heightened emotion had to take place in a completely mundane environment, something even a little tacky. This way the extremity of the moment would stand out in sharp relief to the sheer normalness of the setting. Because it is a public scene, a local news TV studio soon emerged. This way we could show all the major characters—Volumnia, Aufidius, and Virgilia—watching on TV and responding to Coriolanus' public act of self-immolation. Especially, I knew we had to see Volumnia see her son snap, since charting and dramatizing that relationship was central to the storytelling of the movie.

A passing note to screenwriters interested in classical structure: Whenever you come to Act Three in a Shakespeare play, you need to buckle up. This is where the playwright frequently turns the events sharply, using the act as the fulcrum of his five-act story: King Lear's descent into madness on the heath; Iago's lethal manipulation of Othello; the deaths of Tybalt and Mercutio; the assassination of Julius Caesar; Hamlet's "To be or not to be" and Nunnery scene with Ophelia—all Act Three. (Coriolanus' "Cry of common curs" is dead center in the play: Act Three, Scene 3.) When I work, I always try to think of these fulcrum scenes when the balance shifts and the audience has to buckle up: Maximus walking into the Roman Coliseum for the first time in *Gladiator;* Howard Hughes' debilitating plane crash in *The Aviator;* the big Al Pacino/Jamie Fox dinner confrontation in *Any Given Sunday*—all the equivalent of Act Three, Scene 3.

SCENE 47 (CORIOLANUS VOICE OVER)

Here is the second and final use of interior monologue in the movie. These lines are from a scene in the play where Coriolanus says goodbye to his family and friends as he heads out of Rome to banishment. For a while we had that scene in the movie, but cut it to keep the action moving. But we felt we had to hear these lines for a particular reason:

CORIOLANUS (V.O.)
You shall hear from me still...
I go alone,
Like to a lonely dragon.

The poignancy of the word "lonely" in collision with the ferocity and grandeur of the word "dragon" is truly Shakespeare at his best. It sums up the maddening complexity of the character in two words. The dragon image became central for us.

Later in the story, Coriolanus sheds his Roman persona as he joins with Aufidius. He remakes himself into something new. Visually, we wanted to show this transformation. Ralph suggested a tattoo of a dragon. I embraced that and tried to suggest the bizarre cult of personality that grows up around the newly-made Coriolanus—and makes Aufidius jealous. (See also Scenes 59 and 64.) But again, Shakespeare led the way in teasing out the de-humanized dragon imagery. In Act V, Scene IV, Menenius says, "This Martius is grown from man to dragon: he's more than a creeping thing."

SCENE 54 (SHOWER SCENE)

Here was another opportunity to create a dumb-show moment (silent, without words) that would advance our particular take on the play. As noted above, the homoerotic fascination between Coriolanus and Aufidius is deeply embedded in Shakespeare's work:

AUFIDIUS
Know thou
I loved the maid I married; never man
Sighed truer breath. But that I see thee here,
Thou noble thing, more dances my rapt heart
Than when I first my wedded mistress saw
Bestride my threshold.

And again:

AUFIDIUS
Why, thou Mars, I tell thee,

We have a power on foot, and I had purpose
Once more to hew thy target from thy brawn,
Or lose mine arm for it. Thou hast beat me out
Twelve several times, and I have nightly since
Dreamt of encounters 'twixt thyself and me.

So the intense sensuality of Aufidius shaving Coriolanus' head in this scene emerged as a way to show this fascination, as well as the strained intimacy between two warriors, and was meant to mirror the intense sensuality of Volumnia bandaging Coriolanus' wounds earlier. The rawest human responses are never far from the surface in Shakespeare's work; this is one of the reasons his plays are so endlessly modern.

SCENE 67 (MENENIUS' SUICIDE)

Probably the most radical change we made in Shakespeare's play is this scene. In the play, Menenius just disappears from the action. I wanted to resolve his story more dramatically and definitively so created this dumb-show moment. The guilt Menenius must feel, as Coriolanus' political mentor and guide, for his part in the creation of this avenging "dragon" would be profound. So too his realization that Rome is doomed and that his protégé's soul is well beyond redemption. Once he sees the de-humanized Coriolanus he knows he's in a tragedy that is slowly playing itself out. Menenius lacks Volumnia's grim determination: he's too human.

His ending here, quietly slitting his wrists in a sordid landscape of urban blight, seems appropriate for the character and gives a sense of completion in the movie.

SCENE 72 (THE ENDING)

Shakespeare knows how to stick the landing. The endings of most of his plays are breathtaking and bold. I think of heart-rending Edgar in *King Lear:* "We that are young/Shall never see so much, nor live so long." Or Pandarus' nasty curse in *Troilus and Cressida:* "Till then I'll sweat and seek about for eases,/And at that time bequeath you my diseases." Or Prospero's enchanting coda to *The Tempest.* Or the echoing cannons of *Hamlet.*

Coriolanus ends on a somewhat less dramatic note. Aufidius makes a speech on reconciling his emotions about Coriolanus and then his soldiers carry the body off as "a dead march sounded." On stage this is a somber and appropriate ritual that allows the audience to process the events of the violent ending and the entire play. But on screen, we wanted to leave the audience in a state of shock, still grappling with the dissonant emotions of the piece, without the comfort of the stage ritual and music. Ralph and I both wanted the film to end with an exclamation point, not an ellipsis.

We explored many options over the years of developing the movie. I always felt the pull back to Volumnia. I wanted to see her reaction to her son's death. So all the way through filming, the movie ended with Volumnia watching TV: seeing video images of her son's body in the back of a truck. (Like one of those shocking contemporary, almost casual, presentations of death we have become used to on TV and the web.) The screenplay and movie originally ended with a close-up of Volumnia's face and then snapped to black.

But it didn't work. Cutting back to Volumnia in Rome kept adding a new *idea* to what was emerging as a very emotional and intuitive ending. It was a conceit that worked on the page, but not on screen. It required too much *thought* when the *poetry* of the death is just sinking in. We want to stay with the lonely sound of the whistling wind and on Coriolanus. In the editing room in London, Ralph and I explored various versions of the ending with our ace editor, Nicolas Gaster. In the end the sickening image of Coriolanus' corpse being dumped ingloriously in the back of a truck with no ritual or honor was the most powerful last shot. It was a punch to the gut. It made me feel exactly as I feel when I walk out of the production of the play. It is uncompromising.

And finally it stayed true to the organizing principle of the entire movie: follow the character of Coriolanus to the end. His eyes and his story are the movie, even in death.

Q & A

WITH RALPH FIENNES

You've been acting in films for many years. Now you're making your directorial debut as well as starring in **Coriolanus,** *an adaptation of one of Shakespeare's lesser-known plays. Why this film and why now?*

There were two catalysts. The first was playing Coriolanus in a stage production in 2000, and believing that this play of Shakespeare's could become a contemporary, urgent political thriller, with a Greek tragedy at its center, involving the mother and the son. And there's something in the spirit of Coriolanus, in the essence of his character, which spoke to me very strongly and wouldn't leave me.

The other catalyst was Simon Channing Williams, who produced *The Constant Gardener.* We became very close while we were making that movie, and he gleaned that I was interested in directing. In fact, he wanted to produce the first film that I would direct. Very sadly, Simon died. We had tried to get something off the ground, which didn't work. But we had worked on it for two years, and I'd begun to put on the director's hat of scouting locations and so on. That gave me confidence to pick up *Coriolanus* when the other project fell through. Still, I didn't talk about *Coriolanus* to very many people because on the face of it, it seemed unlikely to fly: me as a first-time director, also acting in it, supposedly quote-unquote difficult Shakespeare. Then one day I pitched it, as it were, to my agent, who said, "You should do this."

Coriolanus is dedicated to the memory of Simon Channing Williams, because I know that without his belief in me I might not have had the confidence to move it along.

What drew you to Coriolanus as a character?

I like characters that challenge an audience. With *Coriolanus,* Shakespeare takes a really hard-ass man who despises the people, and makes him the protagonist. Which I think is thrilling, dramatically. Coriolanus comes into the opening of the story and basically tells the people to go fuck themselves. I think we in the audience decide we don't like this guy based on that simple fact. But then the audience experiences him as a soldier, an extremely brave, almost crazy kind of soldier. They come to see that he has a kind of integrity, which is manipulated and destroyed by the world around him, and by his own arrogance and pride. Coriolanus wants recognition and doesn't want it at the same time. He is very riven. I think he's happiest in the battlefield; that's where he is at one with himself.

How did John Logan become involved in writing the screen adaptation?

My agency introduced me to John as the first candidate to write this screenplay. He's a superb screenwriter, and he has an instinctive understanding of Shakespeare's potential on the big screen. I told him my ideas for contemporary *Coriolanus*, and showed him a series of images that corresponded to different stages in the story. He really seemed to understand what sort of film I had in mind and we started to share ideas that would develop it further.

You and John are both known for creatively ambitious work, but each of you also has a long resume of very commercial movies, like **Gladiator** *in John's case and the* **Harry Potter** *series in yours. Did that experience factor in to your collaboration, and how did you work together to develop the script?*

Well, John and I wanted to a make a film that was accessible to a modern audience, and we recognized it needed a strong narrative drive. I'd always found the basic story of *Coriolanus* really thrilling. The play sets up a visceral dynamic of confrontation: between Coriolanus and the audience; between him and the citizens; it develops, as it were, an intimacy of opposites between him and Aufidius; and there is an extraordinary tension between Coriolanus and his mother Volumnia. There are violent battles, power plays, reversals and betrayals. As cinematic storytelling, we felt *Coriolanus* could be exciting and approachable.

Of course, we had to aggressively edit the text. I had already identified some key areas to cut, and John then came up with more cuts and more ways of revising things. He brought great ideas to the table, and he had a fantastic sense of dramatic progression in integrating them into the adaptation.

Were you concerned about a whether a 17th-century Shakespearean play would fit into a modern context?

No, not at all. I believe that Shakespeare is in so many respects extraordinarily modern. Taking aside the question of the language, what's happening in Shakespeare's stories is always relevant—they're *active* as stories. Whether it's a comedy about love; or it's about a young student who can't make up his mind about what he should do about the death of his father; or it's a tragedy about a man who's constantly killing to get his way to the top: everything Shakespeare describes is going on right now. *Coriolanus,* particularly, is always going to be pertinent because the power plays of politics will always be with us.

Side by side with preparing this film, I'd read the newspaper and constantly see variations of events that happen in the story that felt like they came from our film. That's one reason it was important that the film look like today's world, not some indeterminate time period. So, the suits, electronics, cars—they're what we see in our everyday lives. But our "Rome" is not Rome, Italy. Just as the events that happen in *Coriolanus* could happen anywhere, our Rome could be just about city in the world.

Although you set the play in the present day, you chose to maintain Shakespeare's dialogue. Can you explain that decision?

We could have chosen to re-write all the dialogue, but John and I believed that the dialogue should be Shakespeare's. Structurally and in terms of vocabulary, there is an expressiveness and athleticism in the original that, I would argue, you couldn't achieve in modern speech. If you get on board the train, your ear is tantalized and stimulated by how he is framing ideas in conversation. A speech like, "You, common cry of curs whose breath I hate as reeks of the rotten fens/Whose loves I prize like as the dead carcasses of unburied men that do corrupt my air"—the imagery is amazing. How could you possibly translate that into modern vernacular?

Of course, sometimes the language is quite plain and accessible. And when you have actors like Vanessa Redgrave and Brian Cox speaking the lines, it sounds completely natural.

I realize it's a risk; people today are not used to that mode of expression. But I believe that audiences can be delighted and thrilled by what

Shakespeare is doing with dialogue. I guess I'm of the belief that many people like to be challenged. I know I do.

After triumphing over the Volsci, Coriolanus is prodded by Volumnia to seek the office of Consul. In so doing, he's following a tradition that has played out all over the world for centuries. Why do you think people continue to gravitate towards soldiers-turned-politicians, and were there any real-life figures who informed your interpretation of Coriolanus?

I think all countries celebrate the courage of their heroes, though sometimes we get very uneasy when generals start to move into politics. Still, you can look at a character like Ariel Sharon: he had been an extremely tough soldier. But he was elected Israel's prime minister, and whatever your view of him, he was a strong leader, very uncompromising. I think we all recognize that people who are so unwavering and potent in their determination can be very attractive to an electorate. They also can be extremely dangerous. Coriolanus sits right at the nerve center of this ambivalence.

Another person I had in my image book was Vladimir Putin. Because he's uncompromising and, from what I read, his language can be pretty blunt and insulting. He doesn't mince his words. And of course, he's admired and feared.

You said that you view Coriolanus *as a political thriller. What does this story have to say about politics, and how is it relevant to today?*

I think Shakespeare is showing us the continual fickleness of politicians and the people who elect them. This isn't the first time he's dealt with themes of power, and people angling for power and position; it happens in *Richard II* and in *Julius Caesar,* for example. In *Julius Caesar,* as in *Coriolanus,* the spirit and opinions of the people are a crucial element and there, too, people turn on a sixpence. It's arguable that Shakespeare felt that the public is easily manipulated by clever politicians with a gift for speaking, with a gift for turning them around. I think we see that happen in politics all the time. And people grade politicians on every speech that they make. Did he or she nail it or not, did their poll numbers go up or down?

Let's talk about casting and the supporting characters. Coriolanus has been shaped by his mother, Volumnia, and she remains the single most influ-

ential person in his life. Why did you feel Vanessa Redgrave was the right person to play Volumnia?

Vanessa has a profound understanding of life; she brings this to any role she plays. Of course, she's also known as a woman of strong political views and she's uncompromising in speaking her truth. But also, she carries extraordinary gentleness. I thought the mix of iron determination and innate humanity would be incredibly potent.

For me the richness of her performance is actually in its incredible economy and simplicity. At the end, when Volumnia confronts Coriolanus about his plan to attack Rome, it's often performed with the energy of argument. Whereas Vanessa varied it brilliantly, stripping away embellishment so the language and import of the scene became crystal clear. It was extraordinary to play opposite her on that day.

The events of the story are set in motion by a confrontation with the Volscian guerilla force, led by Coriolanus' enemy, Aufidius. Later, Coriolanus will turn to Aufidius when he is banished from Rome. Can you talk a little bit about their relationship?

They're two men who are obsessed with each other. Coriolanus hates Aufidius, but he acknowledges the great warrior that he is. There is an attraction between them. It's the attraction of opposites, and I think it amplifies the obsession and the animosity between them.

There's no question in my mind that Shakespeare wanted to touch on the homoeroticism of combatants, of warriors who are embraced in combat.

How did you cast Gerard Butler?

Interestingly, Gerard's first job ever was in a production of *Coriolanus.* So he knew and loved the play and loved the script. He was very passionate to do it. He brings incredible presence and masculinity and charisma to the role.

Jessica Chastain was fairly unknown when you cast her as Virgilia, Coriolanus' wife.

She had just finished shooting *Tree of Life,* and the film's producer, Bill Pohlad, suggested I meet with her. I immediately thought she was right.

Virgilia's an interesting part. It's not a big part, yet it stands out. Coriolanus calls her "my gracious silence." She's the witness to the horror of what's going on; I think she's silenced by it. Virgilia is the one person in the story who is fully capable of love. Jessica has an extraordinary quality of openness—of goodness, basically—that was absolutely essential for the role.

Were you concerned about taking on the dual jobs of director and star?

Yes, of course. But I never wanted to let go of re-playing the part. I think some part of me felt I hadn't quite fully achieved it onstage. It's a difficult part to play in the theater, because his rage erupts many times and it's challenging, vocally, to find the variation within the rage. But on film I believed the interior life of Coriolanus could be explored and what is not said can be as meaningful as a speech. This is not easily the case on stage.

Can you discuss your choice of Barry Ackroyd as D.P.?

I met Barry on *Hurt Locker*. I only had two days of filming on that movie, but Kathryn Bigelow was very, very full of admiration for him. I think *Hurt Locker* was a tough shoot—long hours, not glamorous conditions at all— and I knew *Coriolanus* would also be demanding. Also, I loved Barry's work on *United 93,* as well as his work for Ken Loach.

Barry comes from a background of documentary, mainly for the BBC. Famously, he's very good at grabbing stuff hand-held, which for battle scenes and crowd scenes was great. And I knew for a lot of these scenes I wanted actors to play the scene through and have Barry weave in and around them. And throughout the shoot, Barry was extraordinary: flexible and alert in the moment to possibilities that I wouldn't have dreamed of. He absolutely got the spirit of what I imagined and took it even further.

Were there any movies you looked to for inspiration?

The one movie we watched was Gillo Pontecorvo's *The Battle of Algiers.* It's shot in black and white and feels like a documentary, very gritty and immediate. The viewer gets the sense of what's going in the street and beyond the street, the danger everywhere, the police presence. That was a definite touchstone for us, particularly with the crowd scenes and the battle of Corioles.

Coriolanus *was filmed in Belgrade, Serbia. How did you come to choose that location?*

I scouted different locations in Eastern Europe. I liked Belgrade because it had the weight of a capital city. It also had a senate chamber, which was a crucial location and which we were able to use in the film. I liked its mix of architecture. You'll see buildings from the Communist era, and 19th-century Austro-Hungarian–style buildings, and then there's very modern glass buildings and office blocks. Belgrade reminded me of lots of cities I've been in —there are bits of London, bits of Brooklyn or Queens, even bits of Shanghai. Again, I wanted the film to feel like it could be set in any city in the world.

How did you find the filming process overall? Did you enjoy it?

I have to say, I loved the process. I loved creating the world of the film. I loved finding the locations, and shooting on location. I was supported by an extraordinary team of people who I felt saved my ass a few times. Barry, the production designer Ricky Ayres, the costume designer Bojana Nikitović, the editor Nic Gaster, the exceptional producers, Gabrielle Tana, Julia Taylor-Stanley, Colin Vaines. And of course the actors?amazing to work with the likes of Vanessa, Gerard, Jessica, Brian Cox, James Nesbitt, John Kani, Paul Jesson, Lubna Azabal, Ashraf Barhom, Dragan Miçanoviç, and the great actor Slavko Stimac (who plays Aufidius' lieutenant). You bring people to the table, and they support you and want to help you realize onscreen what's in your head. It was an amazing experience.

What do you hope audiences take away from Coriolanus?

I hope people come away thinking about the world they're in, and perhaps feeling moved. I didn't want to make a film with a message, and I feel very strongly that Shakespeare's play doesn't give us a message. It presents us with a series of situations, which we are meant to think about. It observes that people want a strong leader when it suits them, but then the next day they'll change their minds because it doesn't suit them. In tragedy, the audience is asked to witness the arc of the hero—his rise and fall—and to reflect on it. Traditionally the tragic protagonist has a flaw which brings them down. In Coriolanus's case, it's his pride. A lonely anger, a monstrous integrity. And I think we see that situation all the time.

ABOUT SHAKESPEARE'S CORIOLANUS

*C*oriolanus, also known as *The Tragedy of Coriolanus,* was written in the latter part of William Shakespeare's career and is his last major tragedy. Like Shakespeare's earlier plays, *Titus Andronicus, Julius Caesar,* and *Antony and Cleopatra,* this play was set in ancient Rome and based on historical accounts. The primary source was the *Life of Caius Martius Coriolanus,* written in the late first century by the ancient Greek historian, biographer and essayist Plutarch. Other possible sources include the Roman historian Livy's *History of Rome.*

Most Shakespearean scholars agree that *Coriolanus* was written directly after *Antony and Cleopatra.* It shares with that play a fascination with the complex private lives of very public individuals. Screenwriter Logan says, "You can see Shakespeare turning over certain themes in this period of his career. In a way, the character of Coriolanus is almost a continuation of the character of Antony: a career military man who is finally brought low by his own shifting conceptions of honor and loyalty. Both Antony and Coriolanus betray their countries, and both are finally undone by their inability to master their intense passions." Shakespeare's exploration of this theme—the isolation and ultimate excoriation of a seemingly popular public figure—would continue in his next play, *Timon of Athens.*

Coriolanus is among Shakespeare's lesser-known plays, but it is hardly without admirers. Poet T. S. Eliot, in his book *The Sacred Wood: Essays on Poetry and Criticism* (1922), called it Shakespeare's "most assured artistic success," along with *Antony and Cleopatra.* Critic and Shakespeare scholar Harold Bloom, in his bestseller *Shakespeare: The Invention of the Human* (1998) writes, "*Coriolanus,* even more than *Julius Caesar* and *Henry V,* is Shakespeare's political play." Citing his fascination with the title character, Bloom describes Coriolanus as "a battering ram of a soldier, literally a one-man army, the greatest killing machine in all of Shakespeare."

Coriolanus is set in the early years of the Roman Republic, which began in 509 B.C. when the tyrannical King Tarquin was overthrown and an elected government took over. Initially, all public offices were open only to the patrician class, who effectively absorbed the absolute power that had been enjoyed by the monarchy. In 494 B.C., ordinary Romans (the plebeians) won the right to elect two representatives, known as Tribunes, to the Roman Senate. But the remainder of Rome's elected offices—including the most powerful office, Consul—remained off-limits to all but patricians, and there was considerable resentment and mistrust between the two classes. Meanwhile, Rome was in ongoing conflict with the Volsci people, who formed a neighboring city-state; the conflict began under King Tarquin and lasted for two centuries.

The historical conflict between Rome and the Volsci and the struggle for political power are woven into the narrative of Shakespeare's play. As the play begins, Rome's plebeians are bearing the brunt of a grain shortage and some citizens are on the verge of revolt. The focus of their anger is the valiant, honorable warrior Caius Martius, a patrician who responds to their complaint with open scorn. Then Rome receives confirmation of an imminent attack by a Volscian army under the command of Martius' blood enemy, Tullus Aufidius, and Martius sets out with a small force for the Volscian city of Corioles. Outnumbered but willing to perish before accepting defeat, Martius conquers the city virtually single-handedly, quashing the Volscian threat.

Upon returning to Rome, Martius is given a third name, Coriolanus, in recognition of his achievement. Pressured by his ambitious mother, Volumnia, the newly- dubbed Coriolanus reluctantly agrees to seek the office of Consul. But he bristles at the rituals of soliciting plebeian votes, and his political enemies, the Tribunes Sicinius Velutus and Junius Brutus, whip up public opposition to his bid. Rejected and banished from Rome, Coriolanus decides to avenge himself on the countrymen who betrayed him. He seeks out his enemy, Aufidius, in the Volscian city of Antium, and offers to join his forces for an attack on Rome. As their armies begin their assault on Roman territories, Coriolanus' closest allies—his friend and political patron, Senator Menenius, and his commanding general, Cominius—vainly implore him to spare the city. Finally, Coriolanus' family—his wife, Virgilia, and son, Martius, along with Volumnia—arrive to beg the avenging warrior for mercy. It is the iron-willed Volumnia, who proudly molded him into a warrior, who has the last word: she wrings from her son the concession that saves Rome. A peace is reached but Aufidius turns on Coriolanus, accusing him of treason. Proud as ever, Coriolanus reacts with fury, daring his enemies to kill him—which they do.

THE WEINSTEIN COMPANY AND HERMETOF PICTURES, MAGNA FILMS AND
ICON ENTERTAINMENT INTERNATIONAL PRESENT IN ASSOCIATION WITH LIP SYNC
PRODUCTIONS LLP AND BBC FILMS A KALKRONKIE LLP PRODUCTION IN
ASSOCIATION WITH ATLANTIC SWISS PRODUCTIONS, ARTEMIS FILMS, MAGNOLIA-
MAE FILMS AND SYNCHRONISTIC PICTURES A LONELY DRAGON PRODUCTION

RALPH FIENNES   GERARD BUTLER   VANESSA REDGRAVE   BRIAN COX

"CORIOLANUS"

JESSICA CHASTAIN   JOHN KANI   JAMES NESBITT
PAUL JESSON   LUBNA AZABAL   ASHRAF BARHOM

Directed by RALPH FIENNES	Executive Producer MARKO MISKOVIC	Editor NICOLAS GASTER
Screenplay by JOHN LOGAN	Executive Producers WILL YOUNG ROBERT WHITEHOUSE	Production Designer RICKY EYRES
Based on the play "Coriolanus" by WILLIAM SHAKESPEARE	CHRISTOPHER FIGG	Composer ILAN ESHKERI
Produced by RALPH FIENNES JOHN LOGAN	Executive Producers NORMAN MERRY CHRISTINE LANGAN ANTHONY BUCKNER	Costume Designer BOJANA NIKITOVIĆ Hair & Make-Up Designer DANIEL PARKER
Produced by GABRIELLE TANA JULIA TAYLOR-STANLEY COLIN VAINES	Co-Producer KEVAN VAN THOMPSON Director of Photography BARRY ACKROYD, BSC	Production Sound Mixer RAY BECKETT, CAS Casting Director JINA JAY

CAST in Order of Appearance
Tullus Aufidius . . . . GERARD BUTLER
Caius Martius Coriolanus . . . . RALPH FIENNES
First Citizen (Tamora) . . . . . . LUBNA AZABAL
Second Citizen (Cassius) . . . ASHRAF BARHOM
Citizens . . . . ZORAN ČIČA
MILOŠ DABIĆ
NICOLAS ISIA
ZORAN MILJKOVIĆ
MARIJA MOGBOLU
MILAN PEROVIĆ
NENAD RISTIĆ
LAWRENCE STEVENSON
MARKO STOJANOVIĆ
TAMARA KRCUNOVIĆ
ZU YU HUA
OLIVERA VIKTOROVIĆ-ĐURAŠKOVIĆ
DANIJELA VRANJEŠ
Menenius . . . . BRIAN COX
Volsce Lieutenant . . . . SLAVKO ŠTIMAC
Young Roman Soldier . . . . . IVAN ĐORĐEVIĆ
1st Soldier. . . . . RADOVAN VUJOVIĆ
2nd Soldier. . . . . . . JOVAN BELOBRKOVIĆ

General Cominius . . . . JOHN KANI
1st Senator . . . . DAN TANA
2nd Senator . . . . . MIODRAG MILOVANOV
Titus Lartius . . . . DRAGAN MIĆANOVIĆ
Volsce Politician . . . RADOSLAV MILENKOVIĆ
1st Volsce Soldier . . . . . RADOMIR NIKOLIĆ
2nd Volsce Soldier. . . . . ZORAN PAJIĆ
Young Martius . . . . HARRY FENN
Virgilia . . . . JESSICA CHASTAIN
Volumnia . . . . VANESSA REDGRAVE
Maid . . . . ELIZABETA ĐOREVSKA
Old Man in Corioles . . . . DUŠAN JANIĆIJEVIĆ
Tribune Brutus. . . . . PAUL JESSON
Tribune Sicinius . . . . JAMES NESBITT
TV Anchorman . . . . JON SNOW
TV Pundits . . . . DAVID YELLAND
NIKKI AMUKA-BIRD
3rd Senator. . . . . ANDREJA MARIČIĆ
4th Senator . . . . SVETISLAV GONCIĆ
Young Senator . . . . UROŠ ZDJELAR
Cleaner in Corridor. . . . . BORA NENIĆ
War Vet . . . . . SLOBODAN BODA NINKOVIĆ
Jamaican Woman. . . . . . . MONA HAMMOND

124

Young Man in Market . . SLOBODAN PAVELKIĆ
Shopkeeper . . . . DRAGOLJUB VOJNOV
TV War Correspondent . . . KIERON JECCHINIS
Camp Barber . . . . MIRKO PANTELIĆ
Stunt Co-ordinator . . . . . . ROWLEY IRLAM
Local Stunt Co-ordinator. . . SLAVIŠA IVANOVIĆ
Stunt Double for Mr Fiennes . . JAMES GROGAN
Stunt Double for Mr Butler . . . . RICK ENGLISH

Stunt Performers . . ROB INCH, NICK MCKINLESS,
MIROSLAV BORKOVIĆ, MILOMIR ČIGOJA,
NENAD ČUDIĆ, BRANISLAV FISTRIĆ, DAVID
GARRICK, VLADAN GOSTILJA, RICHARD
HANSEN, KOSTA JOVIĆ, MARK MOTTRAM,
STANKA PEJOVIĆ DOMINIC PREECE, OGNJEN
RADULJICA, DEJAN SAVOVIĆ DUSAN SAVČIĆ,
ARANĐEL SRETENOVIĆ, MARKO VASILJEVIĆ

Line Producer . . . . ANĐELKA VLAISAVLJEVIĆ
Associate Executive Producers
. . . . ŽIVOJIN ŽIKA PETROVIĆ,
CAROLYN MARKS BLACKWOOD
Post Production Supervisor. . . . . MEG CLARK
Script Supervisor. . . . . . SUSANNA LENTON
Dialogue Coach . . . . . JOAN WASHINGTON
Supervising Production Accountant
. . . . DEBBIE MOORE
Art Director . . . . RADE MIHAJLOVIC
TV Unit Director. . . . . BEN QUINN
Special Effects Supervisor . JASON TROUGHTON
Supervising Sound Editor . . . OLIVER TARNEY
Dialogue & ADR Editor. . . . . SIMON CHASE
Music Producer . . . . . STEVE McLAUGHLIN
Gaffer. . . . . HARRY WIGGINS
End Title Song performed by . . . . LISA ZANE

THIS FILM IS DEDICATED
TO THE MEMORY OF
SIMON CHANNING WILLIAMS

"A" Camera Focus Puller
. . . . OLIVER DRISCOLL
"A" Camera Clapper Loader
. . . . DRAGAN RAKIĆEVIĆ - CILE
"B" Camera & Steadicam Operator
. . . . SVETOMIR PAJIĆ - KIVI
"B" Camera Focus Puller. . DRAŠKO PEJANOVIĆ
"B" Camera Clapper Loader
. . . . BRANISLAV STOJANOVIĆ
Central Loader . . . . ZORAN ŽIVKOVIĆ - ŽIKA
1st Assistant Director . . . . . . ZORAN ANDRIĆ
Key 2nd Assistant Director . . . . VESNA MILIĆ
2nd 2nd Assistant Directors . . LJUBOMIR BOŽOVIĆ,
NIKOLA IVANOVIĆ

Key Set PA. . . . . RADOŠ VUČIĆ
Set Production Assistants . . . TOMO PALIKOVIĆ,
DUSAN POPOVIĆ
Production Managers . . . MIŠKO STEVANOVIĆ,
ALEKSANDAR-LEKA TADIĆ
Supervising Production Co-ordinator . POLLY HOPE
Serbia Production Co-ordinators . ZOJA ĐORĐEVIĆ,
BRANKA CETINA
Production Secretary . . MILICA BREGOVIĆ-TADIĆ
Assistant to Mr Fiennes (UK) . . . ALIX GRAHAM
Assistant to Mr Fiennes (Serbia) . . MAŠA NEŠKOVIĆ
Assistant to Mr Butler . . AMY LOUISE TRIPODI
Assistant to Ms Tana & Mr Vaines
. . . . ZRNKA MIŠKOVIĆ PETROVIĆ
Assistant to Ms Tana (NY) . . ANDREW SEMANS
Assistants to Ms Taylor-Stanley . . IAIN SINCLAIR,
JULIA FESTA
Assistant to Ms Redgrave (Serbia) MILOŠ ĆURČIN
Office Runner . . . . RENATA GRAOVAC
Assistant Location Manager . JASMINA PETROVIĆ
Serbia Production Accountant
. . . . SANDRA ĐURIČKOVIĆ
Serbia VAT Production Accountant
. . . . SRĐAN KRUŠČIĆ
UK Assistant Production Accountant
. . . . DEBBIE PETERSON
Assistant to Serbia Production Accountant
. . . . MILAN KOBALI
Assistant to Serbia VAT Production Accountant
. . . . SANJA ILIĆ
Serbia Cashier . . . . JELENA BEATOVIĆ
Art Department Co-ordinator . . MARIJA NIKOLIĆ
Set Decorator. . . . . LEE GORDON
Assistant Set Decorator . . . . . ALJOŠA SPAJIĆ
Graphics . . . . . ALEKSANDRA MIHAJLOVIĆ
Set Dressing/Prop Buyer. . MARKO DIMITRIJEVIĆ
Chargehand Dresser . . . . . SVETISLAV MADIĆ
Dressers . GORAN MILOŠEVIĆ, MILE NIKOLIĆ,
ŽELJKO BAKIĆ, STANIŠA SAVIĆ,
MILOS TODOROVIĆ, VLADAN DAMJANOVIĆ
Prop Master . . . . RAYMOND MCNEILL
Assistant Prop Master
. . . . ZORAN PETROVIĆ-CRTANI
Stand-by Props . . . . BOŠKO DELIĆ
Assistant Stand-by Props . . . . NUHI TERMET
Art Department Interns . . MILICA MILANOVIĆ,
JELENA RADOVIĆ
Storyboard Artist. . . . . TEMPLE CLARK
Assistant Costume Designer . STEFAN SAVKOVIĆ
Costume Supervisor . ALEKSANDRA KESKINOV
Key Costumier . . . . . . NINA BOGOSAVLJEV
Seamstress. . . . . RADMILA JAKŠIĆ
Costumiers . . . ZORAN KARADŽIC, MARINA
ZARIĆ, MARINA ARSIĆ

Make-Up & Hair Supervisor . . LAURA SCHIAVO
Make-Up Artist . . . . . TINA ŠUBIĆ DODOČIĆ
Make-Up Assistants . . . . . . NATAŠA NIKOLIĆ,
MILJANA PAKIĆ
Prosthetics Scars supplied by . . MARK COULIER
Graphic Artists for Make-up Department
. . . . . IGOR STANGLICKI, NIKOLA PRIJIĆ
1st Assistant Editor . . . . ANDY JADAVJI
Assembly Editor . . . . KIM GASTER
Serbia Assistant Editors . . . . FILIP DEDIĆ,
BILJANA KUNIJEVIĆ
Visual Effects Editor . . . . . KARENJIT SAHOTA
Stills Photographer . . . . LARRY D. HORRICKS
Unit Publicist . . . . CERIS PRICE
Local PR . . . . SANJA VUČIĆEVIĆ
Casting Assistant. . . . . ALEX DUBURY
Serbia Casting Director . . ALEKSANDAR ADŽIĆ,
DANILO BEĆKOVIĆ
Serbia Casting Assistants . . SARA MARINKOVIĆ,
MILANA MILUNOVIĆ
Serbia Casting Agency . . . PAJPER, SLAVA S & R
Crowd Marshall (Serbia). . RADOSLAV VULANOVIĆ
Crowd Marshall (Montenegro). . SLOBODAN IVETIĆ
Chaperones . . . . . NIGEL & CAROLYN FENN
Military Advisor . . . . BARRIE RICE
Sound Maintenance . . . . ST. CLAIR DAVIS
Boom Operator . . . . NEMANJA NOVIČIĆ
Sound Intern . . . . . MIHAILO STEVANOVIĆ
TV Unit Camera Operator. . . MARIJA VUKELIĆ
Video Playback Operators
. . BRANIMIR ŽIVKOVIĆ, MIHAJLO DOBRIĆ
Serbia Gaffer. . . . . . . SLOBODAN GOJKOVIĆ
Best Boy. . . . . SRĐAN GOJKOVIĆ
Lighting Technicians . . . . . MILOŠ VIDAKOVIĆ,
BORISLAV ROMČEVIĆ,
NEBOJŠA SLAVUJEVIĆ
Key Grip . . . . NENAD VASIĆ
Best Boy Grip. . . . . . . ČEDOMIR SUBOTIĆ
Grips. . . . . TRAJČE VELIČKOVSKI,
DRAGAN STEFANOVIĆ
On Set Labour . . . JOVAN VLADIMIR BORKA,
NEVENA POPOVIĆ
Special Effects Co-ordinator
. . . . MUHAMED M'BAREK - TOSKE
Special Effects Technicians . LAURENCE HARVEY,
MARK VANSTONE
Picture Vehicles Co-ordinator . . NENAD KOKOT
Assistant to Picture Vehicles Co-ordinator
. . . . VLADIMIR JOVANOVIĆ
Location Catering . . . . . PARTY SERVICE
On Set Medical. . . . . . ZORICA KUBUROVIĆ
Stunt Rigger and Safety . . . . MILAN ALAVANJA
Transport Co-ordinator . . SLAVKO NOVAKOVIĆ
Transport Captain . . . . . NENAD VELIČKOVIĆ

Mr Fiennes' Driver . . . . . ČEDOMIR ARSEVIĆ
Producers' Driver . . . . ŽELJKO JANKOVIĆ
Unit Drivers (Serbia). . . DRAGAN MUDRINIĆ,
NEMANJA BABIĆ, MIROSLAV TIMOTIJEVIĆ
MIODRAG JOVIČIĆ, NEBOJŠA EREMIJA,
DEJAN JURIĆ, MILAN MILIŠIĆ, ZORAN
ZUBIĆ, MARKO MRDALJ, DUŠAN KREKIĆ,
ZORAN MARKOVIĆ, ZORAN VAGIĆ
DALIBOR MILOVANOVIĆ, IGOR KOKOT,
ILIJA DŽIKIĆ, DEJAN STEFANOVIĆ,
RADOVAN VLAJKOVIĆ, DRAGAN
ŽIVADINOVIĆ, RADIVOJE ĐORĐEVIĆ, SAŠA
BLAGOJEVIĆ, SLOBODAN MARIĆ
Drivers (Montenegro) . . . NOVAK KOPRIVICA,
MARKO MARTINOVIĆ, PREDRAG NEDOVIĆ,
VLATKO NEDOVIĆ, RADOMIR PAJOVIĆ

Additional Photography
Location Manager (London) . . NICK DAUBENY

BBC Newsroom Unit, London
Newsroom Studio Director. . . BARRY THOMAS
Newsroom Studio Technical Manager
. . . . DENIS O'HARE
Newsroom Vision Mixer . . . . SAM SAUNDERS
Newsroom Sound Supervisor. . . . . ANDY COLE
Newsroom Lighting Supervisor . . . . BOB TULLY
Newsroom Floor Manager . . . . . MARK JONES
Newsroom Camera Operator . . . RYAN PHILIPS
Newsroom Studio Service Technician KEVIN KING
Newsroom Hair & Make-Up . . . . . . JO DRAKE
Newsroom Autocue Operator . . ADAM ROBSON
Newsroom Studio Runner
. . . . ALEXANDRA CHARALAMBOUS
Operational Team Leader . . . TANIA GRIFFITHS
Head of Presentation. . . . . . MIKE KAVANAGH

Post Production
Post Production Co-ordinators . AMEENAH AYUB,
TOM WALTERS
Assistant Post Production Co-ordinator
. . . . ELLEN PAYNE
Post Production Assistants . . SHARMILA KUMAR,
STEPHANIE SMITH, AIDAN GROUNDS
Voice Casting . . . . VANESSA BAKER
Clearances. . . . . KATE PENLINGTON
Picture Research . . . . NICOLA BARNES
Archive Researchers . . . . . LUCY WHITTON,
VAL EVANS
For Hermetof Pictures
Legal Services provided by
JOKSOVIĆ, STOJANOVIĆ & PARTNERS
. JELENA IVANOVIĆ, DRAGAN STOJANOVIĆ
OLSWANG, UK . . . . . . JACQUELINE HURT

For BBC Films
Production Executive . . . . JANE HAWLEY
Legal & Business Affairs . . . . SIMON OSBORN
Production & Delivery Co-ordinator
. . . . JAMES BUCKLER
Production Assistant . . . . . . RUTH SANDERS

For Magna Films
Assistant to Executive Producers
. . . . MAGGIE NEWTON
Head of Sales . . . . . CHRISTOPHER LYSTER
LLP Production Co-ordinator . SASKIA THOMAS
Legal Counsel for Kalkronkie
. . . . SAM TATTON-BROWN
Legal Counsel for Magna . . . . . PHIL RYMER

For LipSync Post
PETER HAMPDEN, ROBIN GUISE,
PETER RAVEN
Senior Post Producer - LISA JORDAN
Legal Services provided by
LEE & THOMPSON
NATALIE USHER, REBECCA PICK

Sound Re-Recorded by . . . . . LIPSYNC POST
Re-recording Mixers . . . . . PAUL COTTERELL,
ROB HUGHES
ADR Mixers . . . . ROBERT FARR,
PAUL COTTERELL
Assistant ADR Mixers . . . . BEN TAT,
YANTI WINDRICH
Premix Re-recording Mixer . . . MARK TAYLOR
Foley Editor . . . . GUNNAR ÓSKARSSON
Foley Recordist . . . . ADAM MENDEZ
Foley Artists . . . . JACK STEW, ANDREA KING
Foley Recording . ANVIL POST PRODUCTION

Music Supervisor . . . . IAN NEIL
Musicians Contracted by . . . . . . THE LONDON
METROPOLITAN ORCHESTRA
Trumpet . . . . JOHN BARCLAY
Timpani . . . . TRISTAN FRY
Drums . . . . PAUL CLARVIS
Metal . . . . STEVE McLAUGHLIN
Violin & Cello . . . . ILAN ESHKERI
Orchestration & Copying by
. . JESSICA DANNHEISSER & MILLIE BARING
Music Recorded at . . . NORTHPOLE STUDIO &
BRITISH GROVE STUDIOS
British Grove Engineer . . . . JOE KEARNS
British Grove Assistant Engineer . . JASON ELLIOTT
Northpole Engineer . . . . PAUL SAUNDERSON
Music Mixed at . . . . . . NORTHPOLE STUDIO
Music Mixed by . . . . . . STEVE McLAUGHLIN

Music Co-ordinators . . ELISA KUSTOW & MILLI

Digital Grading by . . . . LIPSYNC POST
Colourist . . . . STUART FYVIE
Online Editor . . . . SCOTT GOULDING
Digital Lab Supervisor . . . . . JAMES CLARKE
Senior D-Lab Operator . . DANIEL TOMLINSON
D-Lab Operators . . . . CHRIS BENTLEY,
ZOE COUSINS, ALBERTO BURON
Technical Support . . . . RICK WHITE,
SALIM RAHMAN,
SCOTT MACBETH
Post Production Engineer . . LINDEN BROWNBILL

Visual Effects by LIPSYNC POST
Executive Visual Effects Supervisor
. . . . SEAN H. FARROW
Visual Effects Supervisor . . . . . ANGELA ROSE
Head of Visual Effects . . . . . STEFAN DRURY
Visual Effects Producer . . SAMANTHA TRACEY
Visual Effects Co-ordinator . . . . . LUCY TANN
Digital Compositors . NAOMI BUTLER, DYLAN
OWEN, SANDRO HENRIQUES, LUKE BUT-
LER NEIL CULLEY, DAVID SJODIN, JOHN
PURDIE, GARETH REPTON
Senior Systems Engineer . . . . . . JON STANLEY

Systems Engineer . . . . YANNI GOUDETSIDIS

Titles and Graphics Designed by LIPSYNC POST
Creative Director . . . . . . HOWARD WATKINS
Senior Designer . . . . JULIA HALL
Graphics Co-ordinator . . . . . OANA ANGHEL

Publicity by . . . . PREMIER PR
CLAIRE GASCOYNE, JONATHAN RUTTER,
MATTHEW DINSDALE
Mr Fiennes' Publicist . . . . SARA KEENE

Costume Hire . . . . . ANGELS COSTUMIERS
Mr. Fiennes' Shoes . . . . BROGUE SHOES
Military Costume Advisor . . . . . . JOE HOBBS
Action Vehicles . . . . . . MIROLSLAV KRSTIĆ,
ARGUS TOURS
Armourers . . . . BOJAN NENADOVIĆ

Studio Facilities . . VISION TEAM, BBC TELEVI-
SION CENTRE, BROADLEY STUDIOS

Facilities Vehicles . . . . CARAVAN METROPOL
Trailers . . . ŽELJKO ĆORAK, PATRICK SURIN,
MLADEN MATIJEVIĆ
Shot with PENELOPE CAMERA & LENSES
(AATON, PARIS)

Additional Camera Equipment
. . . . ICE FILMS, VISION TEAM
Film Stock . . . . FUJIFILM MOTION PICTURE

Electrical Equipment
. . . . PINK FILMS INTERNATIONAL
HARRY WIGGINS . . . .
Grip Equipment . . . . VISION TEAM
. . . .
Editing Equipment HYPERACTIVE BROADCAST
. . . .
Film Processing & Telecine Dailies . . CINELABS &
CINEBOX 100 (MAGIC BOX), BELGRADE . .
UK Telecine Dailies . . . . ARION UK
. . . .
Post Production Laboratory. . DELUXE LONDON
. . . .
DI Laboratory Contact . . . . . . CLIVE NOAKES
. . . .
Travel (Belgrade) . . . . VDV
. . . .
Travel (London) . . . . ET TRAVEL
. . . .

London Extras. 2020
Post Production Script . . . . . . SAPEX SCRIPTS
Dolby Consultant . . . . RICHARD STOCKDALE
Completion Guaranty Provided by
. . . INTERNATIONAL FILM GUARANTORS
LUKE RANDOLPH, EMMA MAGER,
LUCY SMITH
Legal Services Provided by . . LEE & THOMPSON
CHRISTOS MICHAELS, ANWEN GRIFFITHS
MICHAEL ANTONIADES
Auditing Services Provided by. . . . RSM TENON
JOHN GRAYDON, NIGEL WALDE
Insurance Services Provided by . TOTALLY ENTER-
TAINMENT LTD
DEREK TOWNSHEND, DELTA GENERALI
BELGRADE
Collection Account Management by
. . . . FINTAGE CAM B.V

Use of "A Place Calling Itself Rome" a title by John
Osborne courtesy of Gordon Dickerson and The
Arvon Foundation
Archive Material Courtesy of AP ARCHIVE, BBC
MOTION GALLERY, ITN SOURCE, RTS -
RADIO TELEVIZIJA SRBIJE

"ČAJEŠUKARIJE"
(Traditional)
Performed by Goran Bregovic for Kamarad
Production

"FICTION"
(Stephanie Ekwalla / Vincent Guilbert / Florent
Gouriou / Sebastien Herve / Guillaume Rolland)
Performed by Sheer.K
Courtesy of Last Exit Records
By arrangement with RipTide Music, Inc.

"STA PERVOLIA"
(Mikis Theodorakis)
Performed by Lisa Zane
Published Courtesy of Schott Music, Mainz –
Germany
Produced by Steve McLaughlin & Richard Lancaster

Ralph Fiennes would like to thank
JOEL LUBIN, BRYAN LOURD, BRIAN
SIBERELL, ROEG SUTHERLAND, BEN
KRAMER DAN TANA, BILL POHLAD, FRANK
HILDEBRAND, SIMON BERESFORD, JAMES
MIDGELEY, GAIL EGAN, VLADAN MIRKOVIC,
JOSH BERGER, JO CLERKIN, BARRY
THOMAS, BRIAN LEWIS of MEYER & MOR-
TIMER AMANDA HARLECH

The Producers would like to thank
MINISTER OF INTERIOR, REPUBLIC OF
SERBIA - IVICA DAČIĆ
CABINET CHIEF, MINISTRY OF INTERIOR,
SERBIA - BRANKO LAZAREVIĆ
SPECIAL ANTI-TERRORIST UNIT-COMMAN-
DER COL. SPASOJE VULEVIĆ, LT. COL
DRAGAN BARAŠIN
COUNTER TERRORIST UNIT - COMMAN-
DER COL. GORAN DRAGOVIĆ
SPECIAL MILITARY ADVISORS - VLADAN
MIRKOVIC, DEJAN PURTIĆ
MAYOR OF BELGRADE - DRAGAN ĐILAS,
MAYOR OF PANČEVO - VESNA MARTINOVIĆ
MEDIA RELATIONS, MINISTRY OF INTE-
RIOR, SERBIA - SUZANA VASILJEVIĆ
MINISTER OF DEFENCE, SERBIA - DRAGAN
ŠUTANOVAC
PRIME MINISTER OF SERBIA - MIRKO
CVETKOVIĆ
PRIME MINISTER OF SERBIA'S CABINET
CHIEF - MIRJANA JOVASEVIĆ
DIRECTOR McCANN ERICKSON BELGRADE
- SRDJAN ŠAPER
NATIONAL ASSEMBLY OF THE REPUBLIC OF
SERBIA

EXECUTIVE DIRECTOR OF SERBIA FILM
COMMISSION - ANA ILIĆ
DEPUTY DIRECTOR OF USAID (SERBIA
COMPETITIVENESS PROJECT) - SHARON
VALENTINE
NATIONAL MUSEUM OF SERBIA
RTS-RADIO TELEVIZIJA SRBIJE
PUBLIC UTILITY COMPANY "BELGRADE
CITY MARKETS"
THE CITY AND PEOPLE OF BELGRADE
THE CITY AND PEOPLE OF PANČEVO
JANE HAWLEY, JAMES BUCKLER & THE BBC
NEWSROOM

STEVE ALLEN - BARCLAYS BANK, ROY and
LUKE at SGM FOREX
ANDREAS WISEMAN, PAULINE AMOS
BRIONI - ITALY, CHRISTIAN DIOR COU-
TURE - PARIS, MONA D.O.O. - BELGRADE
BROGUE SHOES - EDINBURGH,
ANDREJEVIĆ JEWELLERY - BELGRADE
PRODUCTION SERVICES IN SERBIA AND
MONTENEGRO PROVIDED BY "WORK IN
PROGRESS"
FILMED ON LOCATION IN SERBIA, MON-
TENEGRO AND THE UK

About the Filmmakers

RALPH FIENNES (Director/Producer) has been honored for his work on the stage and on screen. In 2008, Fiennes earned dual British Independent Film Award (BIFA) nominations, for Best Supporting Actor, for his roles in *The Duchess,* opposite Keira Knightly, for which he also received a Golden Globe nomination; and for *In Bruges,* with Colin Farrell. Also in 2008, Fiennes starred in the acclaimed drama *The Reader,* opposite Kate Winslet, and in the six-time Academy Award-winning *The Hurt Locker,* directed by Kathryn Bigelow. That same year, Fiennes received Golden Globe and Screen Actors Guild (SAG) Award nominations for his performance in the HBO movie *Bernard and Doris,* opposite Susan Sarandon. Fiennes was most recently seen reprising the role of Lord Voldemort in the conclusion of the *Harry Potter* series, *Harry Potter and the Deathly Hallows—Part 2.* Fiennes recently completed production on *Clash of the Titans 2.*

A two-time Academy Award nominee, Fiennes received his first nomination in 1994 for his performance in Steven Spielberg's Oscar-winning Best Picture *Schindler's List.* His portrayal of Nazi Commandant Amon Goeth also brought him a Golden Globe nomination and a BAFTA Award, as well as Best Supporting Actor honors from numerous critics groups, including the National Society of Film Critics, and the New York, Chicago, Boston and London Film Critics.

Fiennes earned his second Oscar nomination in 1997 for the title role in Anthony Minghella's *The English Patient.* Fiennes also garnered Golden Globe and two BAFTA Award nominations, as well as SAG nominations, one for Best Actor and another shared with the cast. He later won a British Independent Film Award, an Evening Standard British Film Award, and a London Film Critics Circle Award, and earned a BAFTA Award nomination, for his work in the acclaimed 2005 drama *The Constant Gardener,* directed by Fernando Meirelles.

Fiennes additional film credits include; *Cemetery Junction; Nanny McPhee and the Big Bang; Clash of the Titans; The White Countess; Wallace and Gromit and the Curse of the Were-Rabbit; Red Dragon; The End of the Affair; The Good Thief; Spider; Chromophobia; Onegin; Sunshine; Maid in Manhattan; The Prince of Egypt; The Avengers; Oscar and Lucinda; Strange Days; Quiz Show;* and *Wuthering Heights,* in which he made his feature film debut.

A graduate of the Royal Academy of Dramatic Art, Fiennes began his career on the London stage. He joined Michael Rudman's company at the Royal National Theatre and later spent two seasons with the Royal Shakespeare Company (RSC). In 1995, Fiennes opened as Hamlet in Jonathan Kent's production of the play, winning a Tony Award for his performance when the production moved to Broadway. He reunited with Kent in the London production of *Ivanov,* later taking the play to Moscow.

In 2000, Fiennes returned to the London stage in the title roles of *Richard II* and *Coriolanus.* In 2002, he originated the role of Carl Jung in Christopher Hampton's *The Talking Cure* at the Royal National Theatre and, the following year, played the title role in Ibsen's *Brand* at the RSC. Fiennes played Mark Anthony in Deborah Warner's 2005 production of *Julius Caesar,* before reuniting with director Jonathan Kent to star in Brian Friels' *Faith Healer.* The play opened in 2006 in Dublin and later went to Broadway, where Fiennes earned a Tony Award nomination for his performance. In 2009, Fiennes opened in the Yasmina Reza play *God of Carnage* in London's West End and then starred in Kent's production of *Oedipus* at the National Theatre.

JOHN LOGAN (Screenwriter/Producer) received the Tony, Drama Desk, Outer Critic Circle, and Drama League awards for his play *Red.* This play premiered at the Donmar Warehouse in London and at the Golden Theatre on Broadway. He is the author of more than a dozen plays, including *Never the Sinner* and *Hauptmann.*

His work as a screenwriter includes *Hugo,* as well as *Rango, Sweeney Todd* (Golden Globe award), *The Aviator* (Oscar, Golden Globe and WGA nominations), *Gladiator* (Oscar, Golden Globe and WGA nominations), *The Last Samurai, Any Given Sunday,* and *RKO 281* (WGA award, Emmy nomination).